WINDOWS PHONE FOR EVERYONE

A Guide for Everyone Who Wants to Set Up, Learn and Master Windows Phone devices Covering Windows Phone OS v7, v7.1 and v7.5

Diego M. Samuilov

WINDOWS PHONE FOR EVERYONE

A GUIDE FOR EVERYONE WHO WANTS TO SET UP, LEARN AND MASTER WINDOWS PHONE DEVICES COVERING WINDOWS PHONE OS V7, V7.1 AND V7.5

By Diego M. Samuilov

Printing History:

April 2012, First Edition

ISBN-13: 978-1468112115

ISBN-10: 1468112112

This Book Is Dedicated To My Dad,

Leo Samuilov

He Introduced Me To My First Computer When I Was A Kid.

Table of Contents

Acknowledgments

I would like to thank my wife; Maria Veronica, my sons Patrick and Mark, my parents, my sister and my brother. I am very thankful for the family I have; to them I thank for their love, patience and support in all my endeavors.

I am especially thankful to my Dad; who introduced me to my first computer and I know is watching down on me. The hobby you saw start with a small home computer in 1985 took a whole life of its own. I particularly treasure my conversations with my Mom at the end of many long workdays. I believe this is where I learned how to explain technical concepts in non-technical terms.

I would like to give special thanks to my good friend Leandro Olivestro; who was my mentor in my early professional life as a consultant.

All of my friends, who also deserve a big "thank you" for their suggestions, opinions, help and putting up with my being such a geek.

About The Author

Diego Samuilov has worked in Microsoft's environments since he started his professional career in 1990. Since then, he has been through all possible positions related to the Software Development lifecycle: he has held positions as a developer, analyst, technical lead, project lead and auditor. He has a broad experience in the application development arena and since 1996 as a project manager for projects in the Server, Desktop, Web and Mobile environments. He enjoys the software development process which has played a great part in his skills development.

He still likes to keep part of the projects he leads for designing and developing himself so that he can keep his technical skills up to date.

Since the introduction of Windows CE in the late 1990s he has been involved in one form or another in the development of several solutions for the mobile environment. He participates in public and private developer community events. He actively collaborates with the community at support forums and blogs.

His management experience started when leading small development teams as a Lead Developer. Even as an executive, he has always been a "very hands-on" manager with a high level of participation in the development functions. He has experience in IT Management since 1996, when he started as a Senior Analyst and Solutions Integrator, while working for a consulting company.

He currently holds an Information Technology Executive position while at the same time writes for his blog Gadgetix.com.

Preface

Introduction

Windows Phone is here to stay. It was initially released in November of 2010. Slowly but surely it has been gaining market share. Less than a year later, the platform was being projected by independent market analysis companies to become one of the top players in the area. These projections from Gartner and IDC show Windows Phone displacing RIM's Blackberry platform from the third place in market share in 2013; and even displacing Apple's iPhone from the second place in market share worldwide by 2015.

Windows Phone is here to stay and proof of that is the rich variety of apps available in the App Marketplace. Windows Phone's App Marketplace is growing at a pace faster than the Android Market's app store historically did less than a year after being released.

Additionally, Microsoft is launching a wave of updates on all its platforms where they will all become more consistent with each other. Windows 8 and its game console (the Xbox 360) will have a similar user experience to that of Windows Phone. This consistency will help users who learn one platform benefit and even come to expect certain behavior from the other platforms. The learning curve of this user interface is shorter and much easier to understand. Additionally, learning one platform will help you learn the idiosyncrasies of the others. Even though they are built for different functions, they are supporting each other on features that are handled in very similar ways.

It is easy to justify why you need to read this book: you need to learn the user interface for 2012's release of Windows 8, and Windows Phone is a great training tool for the Operating System that will come installed in more than 90% of PCs in the coming years... not to mention the expected upgrade for most of the 1.25 billion PCs already being used. In the process of learning how to use this cool and attractive phone OS; you will enjoy an easy to use interface that will help you achieve your daily tasks no matter where you are.

This book allows you to learn quickly and in an organized way pretty much everything you can do right out of the box. Additionally, it also suggests and explains some of the third party apps (some of which are free) that you can use to complement your experience and become a more productive person on the go.

Third party research NPD claimed in September of 2011 that 44% of current and future US smartphone owners were considering Windows Phone 7 smartphones. The study goes on to reflect on the simplicity of the OS and its contrast with Android OS smartphones. Usability has become a key enhancement in the many releases of Android. However, its inherent complexity remains as the primary reason why many first time users of Android are moving to other platforms. Users of Android OS are moving into this growing platform in increasing numbers to a point where Microsoft is expecting to sell in excess of 600 million device licenses in 2015.

Who Should Read This Book?

This book is intended for technical and non-technical people. In the current market; everyone is a potential user of a smartphone. Smartphones can help anyone:

- from the soccer-mom that wants to stay up to date with news she has no time for at home, organizing her kids' schedule along with her own
- to the technologically challenged that wants to learn how to use a smartphone
- to the non-technical company employee that was just handed a company-sanctioned smartphone
- to the retiree that wants to know how these little gadgets work-and-oh-by-the-way update the old cellphone
- to the company executive willing to get a smartphone that has no compromises while being safer than other options in the market
- to the independent professional willing to get good complementary documentation for the new smartphone

- to the smartphone enthusiast that is excited to get the newest shiniest smartphone OS out there

If you fit into any of these profiles, you are planning/thinking about purchasing a Windows Phone or you have just purchased a Windows Phone; then this book is ideal for you. You will be able to either learn as you go or prepare before you make the switch. In the end you will find that this is an easy flowing book that will help you move as fast as you are willing to read.

If you are an advanced user, this book is also for you and can work as a manual. If you find yourself looking for a specific feature or how to make better use of it, then this book will more likely explain to you how to do so.

What Does This Book Cover?

This book is divided in chapters that increase in complexity as you get deeper into the features that Windows Phone has to offer. I have made every effort to revise and make sure that the content of this book is explained in a way that you will understand. Reading this book will not require you to be a smartphone expert. In an attempt to ensure the terms are provided as clear as possible while making no assumptions of your technical level, I will make myself available via my blog http://gadgetix.com to answer any questions you have about the content in this book.

This book is designed to work in three different ways:

- Read-and-experiment for learning bit by bit and trying things out on your phone. This method will be particularly beneficial for users who never used a smartphone or would rather make sure they try everything they read and learn by experience.
- Read beginning-to-end for a learning experience that will help you use your phone. I particularly recommend this option for users who feel more comfortable with technology and will come back to the book mostly for consultation purposes.

- Manual: Although this book is no Windows Phone manual at all, it is detailed enough to be used for consultation purposes. Use this book as your source for trying to learn how to take better advantage of your phone on specific areas you may not be familiar with.

Following is a quick review of all chapters that will help you jump directly into each section if you are not reading this book beginning-to-end.

Contents

Chapter 1: How Will The Phone Experience Be?

In this chapter I describe what you should expect from the UX (user experience) with Windows Phone. Should you be intimidated by a new type of phone? What does it look like? Is this smartphone OS difficult? Can I test-drive it anywhere? If you are a beginner, should you try it? If you are an advanced or power user, is this a feature rich platform for your advanced needs?

Chapter 2: Preparing The Field

This is the chapter where we setup some online services for you to use from your phone. Your Windows Phone works at its best when fully online. Windows Phone gets all the information it needs from different services. Setting them up before you start up your smartphone will get you going faster and will help you see and understand how everything works right away since all the information will appear into your phone at the time of activation.

Chapter 3: Choose The Best Phone For You

Have you chosen the Windows Phone that best fits you? If you have not purchased your Windows Phone, now it is the time to do so. This chapter covers some of the features that make each Windows Phone device stand up and differentiate itself from the other Windows Phones in the market.

Chapter 4: Initial Setup – A Step By Step Guide

So you purchased a Windows Phone, now what do we do? This chapter takes you through the few steps it takes you to get up and running with a connected smartphone. You will setup a minimum of services to get you running, but this will cover email and social networks plus some of the basic workings of Windows Phone. If you start playing around with the included features, after completing this chapter you will know how to move around the settings and other features offered by Windows Phone OS.

Chapter 5: A Phone In The Cloud

What does it mean to be fully connected all the time with your smartphone? How did Microsoft make sure you benefit from an implementation "In the Cloud"? How does this implementation compare to other online offerings? Do you need to worry about backups and syncs? This chapter also reviews what Microsoft offers for free with the My Phone website.

Chapter 6: Your Windows Phone As Your Social Guru

Windows Phone OS focuses on making you the center of your social network. How is this achieved? How can you take advantage of these features and save time in the process of checking a million status' and social network feeds. Can you benefit professionally from using a smartphone that centers its focus on social networks so much? Find out how to streamline your communications with some of your professional relationships with the social features offered by Windows Phone OS. Your will also learn how to use your device to go to a single place and check the social feeds from all your family members or your closest friends by using groups and other features.

Chapter 7: Your Windows Phone – Preinstalled Apps

This chapter covers all the apps that come as part of your Windows Phone OS. These apps behave the same way on all your Windows Phone devices and regardless of the manufacturer, giving all the platform tools a consistency not seen in any other mobile platform. You can go through this chapter to see how a particular app works or to learn the fine details on each of these apps.

Chapter 8: Settings

This chapter will cover everything there is to know about how to setup your Windows Phone. All settings that control the behavior of your device or how the preinstalled apps work will be explained here. Even though most settings are self-explanatory; you will be able to see a detailed description of what each setting does; what are the most convenient settings to keep and why it is more convenient to keep them that way.

Chapter 9: The Windows Zune Software

In this chapter you will learn how to install the Zune Software and use it to sync your desktop with your Windows Phone. Other features offered by the Zune software are also described, so you will also see how to play, collect, purchase or download music, video, podcasts and apps through this great complement to your Windows Phone device.

Chapter 10: Expand Your Windows Phone

This chapter will give you a few examples of the apps you can use to expand your Windows Phone's capabilities in ways that may surprise you. This is not where your device's expansion capabilities end, in fact; as the Windows Phone Marketplace grows; you are bound to find more and new ways in which to use your Windows Phone.

Chapter 1: How Will The Phone Experience Be?

Easy, consistent, polished, relevant, without glitches... if there is one word to describe it, it should be "smooth"... "very smooth". Well, I guess that really makes it more like 3 words!

User setup is easy, you are up and running in no time, your contacts are yours... they are kept on the web and backed up continuously from your phone to your Live account (which you can reuse if you already have one or create brand new if you don't).

Your carrier may even offer you to transfer your contacts from your old phone into your new one for a fee or you can do that yourself. You will be up and running with the very basic immediately. After a day or two, you will be able to do most tasks. After that, it will be up to you and it will depend on how fast (or slow) you want to move.

In my experience non-technical users are up and running in almost no time. This platform and the user experience are so consistent throughout that it is very easy to get used to it.

Anyone who already has a Passport-enabled email account (Hotmail, MSN, Live, etc.) can just plug in their credentials (username and password or email and password) into a new Windows Phone and all their contacts start to come up on their phone; if they have accounts with Facebook, LinkedIn, Twitter, etc. they can also do the same and see how their contacts start showing up on their phones. For people who have never used Windows Phone, generally, this is the moment their faces change expression, they light up. The phone becomes "theirs" by just entering a username and a password.

Windows Phone is so deeply integrated with social media that you can just as easily call or text someone as you can chat in Facebook or post a picture on your wall. This is the first truly socially-networked phone... it has been so since Windows Phone OS was initially released in November 2010. This is so much the case that since then, all major smartphone OS vendors have scrambled to integrate to social networks with different degrees of success. Some have blatantly copied the way the integration works others have come up with workarounds but none has been able to integrate social networks so deeply into the OS as Microsoft has done.

All in all, your experience will be the most pleasant experience you ever had with a phone. Simple, yet powerful; you will be able to complete your tasks at hand in just a few touches of the screen.

The phone has such as polished user interface that you can see how different your other phones were before this one. Everything about this phone OS is consistent and well thought out. Microsoft has outdone itself on this OS and the results are so well received by critics and users that it encouraged them to reproduce the same type of experience in their next generation desktop OS: Windows 8.

Try It Before You Buy It

Don't even try to take my word for it… go to a store, whichever carrier you like the most and ask them to demo a unit for you. Don't accept those plasticky/non-functioning phone shells they have at most stores; instead ask that someone that knows how to use it to show you how it looks after they set it up and how they personalized it. You may not want to personalize it in that same way yourself, but at least you will see what your possibilities are.

Microsoft had some PR problems with the salespeople that were supposed to know about the OS. The biggest mistake Microsoft made in this whole platform rollout in 2010 was to assume that everyone would be prepared with the details of the new OS. What has happened is that many salespeople have assumed that it is just a new release from their older mobile OS (Windows Mobile) when in fact it is nothing like it. Salespeople selling Windows Phones should know better, if they don't, just insist that they show you one working, or simply ask for the store manager: you are the customer, you know what you want; make yourself heard. Please remember that you may not get the exact same unit that you are being demoed so, do not enter your username and password to any of the social sites or services on that phone.

Once you become more of an advanced user, you will start downloading free apps or even purchasing apps here or there. Most apps are either free; free (with a banner add at the bottom) or are paid. The ones that are paid are mostly under $2 - $3. Some may be a bit more expensive, but the same "try it before you buy it" principle stands, they offer "trial" versions that are either fully functioning and expire after a given amount of days. If that is the case you can always purchase it if you like it and you feel you will end up using it. Don't feel intimidated by the number of apps you can try… pace yourself and try as many as you want; who knows, you may end up finding a real gem.

Minimalistic Design – The Metro UI

The name of the design language or style that the Windows Phone OS has today is called "Metro UI", this is a user interface that is centered on a design language based on typography that slides, fades and moves on screen. If the way Windows Phone looks familiar to you, this is not a coincidence; Microsoft has chosen to use the same design principles that are normally used in graphics you can find in airports, bus, railway, subway and "metro" stations. This innovative approach to a software user interface "clicks" with most people, simply because we are used to using these signs to orient us in our daily life. We use these "user interface" in real life, even if we are not familiar with that physical place we are in. The Metro UI uses a typography that looks familiar. It combines text with bold and multi-culturally obvious icons in few contrasting colors which ends up making a perfect design case for software easy to learn. Font weight and size have a specific meaning in this design language. A larger/bolder font size will indicate more important set of information than a smaller font size being laid out on screen.

The Windows Phone OS user interface is not the first use of this design language. However, it is the most refined use of it up to date. Some of its predecessors are Windows Media Center; the "living room" version of Windows XP, later converted to an application included in other releases of Windows. Microsoft Zune; a portable media player/MP3+Video+Radio player that was launched in the mid-to-late-2000's had a very early version of the UI that Windows Phone has today. The user interface in both of these cases was rougher around the edges than Windows Phone OS is today. The Xbox 360 game system was updated with a very similar Metro UI in the fall of 2011, moving the Xbox 360 to this new paradigm.

Moving forward you will see in 2012 that Windows 8 for PCs will be released using the same Metro UI style with the same minimalistic approach. Windows 8 will support right off the box; desktops, laptops, ultra-books, tablets and lightweight tablets with gestures on touchscreens and the use of more traditional input forms such as mice and keyboards. In any case, regardless of the input method, the mechanics of the style and general user interface will still be consistent across the different platforms.

Everyone will be in touch with some form or another of Metro UI system. Whether it is at work in your Windows 8 desktop, laptop or tablet; or if you are a gamer using Xbox 360 or you are a Windows Phone OS user, you will be in touch with this revolutionary and innovative user interface. But don't despair and try not to feel intimidated by change. This is a very natural interface where you will learn the basics pretty quick no matter how technical (or non-technical) your background is.

Consistency is the key here... while other platforms struggle with UI fragmentation, Microsoft is making sure its users can leverage what they learn in one platform to be used in all other platforms they support.

Some of the key Microsoft competitors are ranging from struggling to make their experience consistent to not caring at all. Here are some examples:

- Mac OS vs. iOS: The UI is not consistent at all simply because Apple dictates that their devices should not be used for the same task, yet we see people using Macs for producing and consuming media of all kinds; iPads to produce and consume media of most kinds and iPhones also being used to produce and consume media of most kinds... However, no matter how successful these platforms are, they are not consistent across the board, and users suffer for it having to learn how to use each device on their own.
- Android OS: the leading smartphone platform and number two in the tablet market is struggling with extreme fragmentation across all their brands with a

very inconsistent UI experience. Users attempt to jump from one manufacturer to another and are finding themselves with a completely different interface. This makes a difficult platform to learn even more difficult.

- Rim's BlackBerry platform does not cover the PC market and was very strong in the smartphone arena. In the last few years they have released a tablet that has struggled to gain market share. Unfortunately their internal struggle and indecision about what they will do with their OS upgrades has literally scared away the few developers they had working on their platform. To make matters worse, their first version of their tablet OS did not even have an email client!

Easy For Basic Users

Windows Phones using Metro UI are ideal for basic users. The basic functions can be learned in a few hours of normal use. The mechanics are straightforward and use simple gestures on the touchscreen that come across as very natural.

Windows Phones can take pictures almost instantly; they are the fastest phones that will go from pocket to picture to social media. The competitors are simply not up to par in this area. These smartphones pass the "mother test" and the "grandmother test" where you can hand in these phones to your mother or grandmother and with about a 2 minute tutorial you can have them up and running. While this does not add too many points to the "cool factor"; they certainly make one hard-to-beat-platform. Try giving your grandmother an Android phone! You can be certain that she will take a while to even figure out how to answer the phone, work those widgets, even worse; do you think she will get to the browser and access the web?

One thing that is extremely cool about this Windows Phone is that most apps take advantage of what is known as "live tiles" instead of just an icon with a static image. This means that right on the first screen, you have most information you need. You can use a weather tile showing you all the information you need without having to even open the app. All apps can be pinned to the home screen and even better, most apps sub-screens can be "pinned" directly. This means not only that you can have a shortcut of sorts pointing into your application but you can have a specific screen of your application being pointed into.

Making your phone truly yours is one of the best features this phone OS has. You have the ability to pin contacts to the home screen, let's say I am pinning my wife's contact into my home screen. This will cause a live tile to appear on the home screen. It will switch back and forth from her name to her picture. Mind you, this is not a picture I have to keep about her… this is the latest picture she posted to any number of social networks. The phone goes out and picks up the latest picture from any of those social networks and shows it in a very friendly way. Most of the time, when I am working, I notice that her picture has changed on my home screen. This usually means that she recently uploaded a picture to her Facebook page. One tap on her tile and I am reading all the comments listed for that picture from our friends. And I am not even opening the Facebook app yet! Other things that will cycle through on her tile are the latest comments she wrote on Facebook (but not the replies). Most of the information you'll need is essentially available on your Windows Phone home screen.

Ultimately, this "Live Tile" functionality is what makes your phone truly YOUR PHONE. You are no longer just displaying your apps on your phone, but information about what matters the most to you. Your phone becomes you; it reflects who you are and no longer just what you can do with it.

Windows Phone creates a great experience by seamlessly integrating content that comes from all kinds of services on the web. Content coming from feeds in Live, Facebook, Twitter, LinkedIn, etc. are all aggregated and fed into your phone showing you things as simple as the latest picture from your contact on any of the social networks or even any news or comments from any of your contacts.

To a user who feels like a beginner with smartphones, this will seem to be an advanced feature, but I am certain you will be able to do this right off the box when you setup your phone the first day. Get past that initial intimidation that you may feel for buying a new gadget and focus on enjoying the experience. Regular usage cannot "brick" your phone (make your phone unusable). Play with it, experiment with the settings… you don't need to setup any social network or email account on it other than your Live Passport account, but the more accounts you setup, the more the phone will be "like you".

Even if you are able to do this and more; you may feel a bit intimidated with the amount of things and accounts you want to setup on your phone. Don't worry; everything about this smartphone OS is where it is expected to be. After a few hours with your phone, you will be able to move around your screens with ease. Just turn on that adventurous attitude and get into any app you want. Worst case scenario, you can always hit the "Windows" logo/button on the front of your phone and you will be sent back to your home screen or you can take a few steps back by tapping on the "Back" button just left of the Windows button.

If you need help, don't worry, this book will help you through every step until you become an expert. And that will happen in no time. Still if you need further help you can always write me a line or two at http://gadgetix.com

Easy For Advanced Power Users

Most people would think that because this smartphone OS is easy for beginners and inexperienced users this platform is not likely to suit them. While this may be true for other platforms, it is so not the case with Windows Phone OS! This is a platform that increases functionality as you get to know it better and take advantage of functions that may not be so obvious to beginners but are still available to you.

Another example I have seen of this was in one of the early previews of Windows Phone OS 7.5. In this case an app created by an airline was presented. You download the free app into your phone. You can pin the app into your home screen like so many other smartphone OS but this is not the end of it. Once you go through the initial entering of your miles program code (or your airline's website user name and password), the application will display all your reservation information in one screen; all your flights on the other and so on… The best thing about it is that you can pin each of these screens into your home screen. Ultimately you can create three or four tiles for each of these internal screens and the tile will display the information regarding your next flight in one tile, the information about your reservations on another and your delays, gates, or additional information on the other tiles. So, let's assume that you are on the previous day to leaving for a week-long business trip or vacation, multiple connection flights, the whole deal: you download the app to your phone, pin into your home screen your different pages from the app and you're set for your whole week. Any changes to your flight schedule will be obvious to you. No more missed flights, waiting at the wrong gate, or just missing it for being distracted!

But what happens if you do not have a miles plan from that particular airline?

Simple: browse your own airline website from your Windows Phone browser (IE in Windows Phone 7 can browse with the same features as IE7 and IE in Windows Phone 7.5 can browse just like the desktop version of IE9), and then all you need is to tap on "pin to start" on your Windows Phone browser and you have a "shortcut" to that particular webpage, if you set it to remember your login and password, you won't even need to login into it and will be able to get to the information on a single tap.

Of course, the most advanced features may require more than a single step, but that is not necessarily the case; in some of these cases, they may just require a few extra steps to complete that a beginner may not necessarily remember. A hurdle easy enough to get by within the first few tries. If you are technically savvy, even within other environments, you will find the basics a breeze to get used to. Additionally, you will get in touch with the advanced settings easily.

If you are a power user or an advanced user, then you like to get into settings and experiment just to see what happens. Windows Phone has all settings well organized and grouped by feature type. Go to settings and you will have access to all of the possible system settings available to your phone's OS. Slide sideways from system settings and you have immediate access to the settings to all the apps that come bundled with your Windows Phone. Each downloaded third party app (even the ones from your carrier and/or smartphone manufacturer) may have their settings section within the app. These settings will affect only the behavior of the app.

What a miracle!
Battery Life Expectancy

On any regular weekday, you can leave home for the day and not come back until late at night. Is it unreasonable then, to expect that a phone that goes with you and stays with you should have a battery that lasts through that day? I don't think so.

The establishment has tried hard to let us know that as long as we want more processing power, we should expect batteries to last less because more powerful processors use, quite naturally, more power. On the surface, this seems a very reasonable statement. However, the number one reason for depleting your battery is your screen when on at all times. This is easily resolved by timing out the screen to a lower setting and even turning it off when not necessary (for example while on a call and you have your device next to your ear). Device manufacturers have even come up with sensors that detect how much ambient lighting there is and therefore setting the brightness to whatever is necessary as opposed to an arbitrary setting. The second item that draws battery power the most is (not how fast but) how much processing is done. I don't mean to say that our devices process too much; but how much unnecessary is done at a single time. If I was assuming that all programming is perfectly done, it has no bugs at all and no one programs their code by cutting corners, I may not have a point. But then again; mobile OSs release cycles are down to several iterations a year; application software can be automatically updated. The end result is that developers tend to lower the guard and some come dangerously close to negligent levels. Here is how Microsoft has been able to protect itself against these cases and how its main competitors have failed.

Sometimes the OS allows too much access without being able to have everything under its control; such is the case of Google's Android OS. The OS allows any number of apps and services to run at the same time. Great for multitasking you might think... but the problem is that everyone leaves their app running so it is readily available when the user wants to come back to it; even if the user never intended to come back. Additionally, there are lots of tools that launch themselves as services: again, great for availability. End result: your device is processing more than it should be processing, your device has so many services and apps running on its own background that it eats up battery for excessive processing when you hardly needed it. The only solution in sight is the appearance of third party tools called "App Killers", which (again!) stays up running in the background checking what is running and "kill" every app not listed as "allowed" in order to extend battery life. While not certainly all of Google's fault, app developers are also to blame because they are not looking at the consequences of their actions.

Sometimes, the urgency to release an OS to market on an arbitrary date is all that counts. Such seems to have been the case of Apple's iOS 5. While it was great to see how Siri handles voice questions. It turned out to be just smoke and mirrors because the most expected item out of a mobile OS is that it should survive a whole day of usage. iOS v5 on the iPhone 4S turned out to be horrible on battery life. The update that supposedly fixes battery life (iOS 5.0.1) turned out to be even worse as some have reported back and forcing Apple to immediately get back to work on the release of more iOS

Everyone fixes and patches, particularly Microsoft has had its own share of issues and missteps in the past, however when they took their time to release a new OS for smartphones; they took enough time to make the right decisions. Windows Phone OS is an incredible multitasker while keeping total and absolute control of what is running under the hood. Windows Phone OS "freezes" apps as they go into the background and then restarts them so they can work whenever it deems necessary (or reasonable). The end result is a multitasking OS that runs as many apps as needed in the background while not using too much battery, memory and resources.

Additionally while smartphone OS user interfaces (UIs) get refreshed multiple times a second to display forms and objects, they are becoming more power hungry. While every other smartphone OSs UI have consistently become more complex, with more shading and color gradients being displayed on screen and shading for buttons and other objects; the Metro UI has made Windows Phone extremely easy on processing, therefore; easy on battery life. This has made such a powerful statement that Microsoft is shifting all of their OSs to the Metro UI to take advantage of all the benefits it can get from this paradigm shift: more power efficient, easier to learn, ensuring consistency across multiple OSs and ensuring consistency on third party applications.

Windows Phones can run just as powerful processors as their competing OSs, but while having several times longer battery lives.

A Smartphone Made For Calling Too?

Windows Phone OS is a social phone, it lets you run apps, it connects you online and it lets you do all the things you can do with the competing OSs all that and more such as the exclusive Xbox LIVE gaming experience and the exclusive Microsoft Office features. All these plus it does not diminish or hide the one feature why this device is called a phone; it uses all the features it can to make calling a better experience. By integrating the social features into the phone OS itself, it makes calling a better experience!

Chapter 2: Preparing The Field

How do I transfer from other mobile devices?

This is the number one reason why most people do not upgrade their smartphones as often as the manufacturers want. You have to go through copying all your contacts from your old phone to the new one. On smartphones, there are several ways to get past this hurdle. If you have your contacts in your old phone and want to transfer them to your new one, you can do one of several things.

- When transferring from a GSM feature phone (any cell phone that is not a smartphone that uses a SIM card), you can have your contacts transferred to the SIM card. When you place the SIM card in your new Windows Phone, those contacts will become available to you as well. If you have done this in the past; this will be exactly the same as the last time you did this; only this will be the last time you do it.
- If your carrier uses CDMA technology: Verizon, Sprint, Metro PCS and others in the US; the rest of the world has pretty much moved on to newer cellular technologies; they do not use SIM cards to transfer contacts. You can go to the nearest cell phone company store and ask them to transfer the contacts from one phone to the other. They have the devices to do so, or will give you the software you need to connect your old cell phone to your computer and from there you can access your information.
- Some carriers offer a service where your contacts stored on your phone can be accessed online as a backup. These services normally allow for exporting contacts so you can use them on your other services or online. You may be charged for this option; save a few dollars and take this opportunity to learn your new smartphone's features.

Get a Passport or Windows Live ID

As mentioned before, Windows Phone will aggregate from a series of services online and will create a unique experience based on the information coming from those feeds. The aggregation happens online with a service that identifies your settings. The set of credentials (user name and password, or email and password) are tied to a Windows Live ID, formerly known as a Windows Passport, Live Passport, MSN Passport, or simply Passport, or Windows ID.

You may already have a Passport and not realize it: all of Microsoft services online and some third party vendors use Passport as a generic way for you to certify you are who you say you are. I am not going to list all Passport sites, but if you have an email from Hotmail, MSN, Live, Windows Live, or you use services from Zune, Xbox LIVE, Windows Messenger, Live Messenger, MSN Messenger, Passport.com or any other popular online services based on Microsoft credentialing, you already have a passport. You do not need to create one. If you don't, then start by creating an account at Live.com. The process is simple and it only requires that you choose a username that hasn't been chosen yet, a password and provide some additional demographic information which will not be used for other purposes than to provide you with localized information.

Please note that if you do not want to provide real and factual demographic information, you could very well do so. You could even chose not to setup a Live ID account, but that would prevent you from having access to those services online and even having a real-time backup of your smartphone's contacts, calendar, emails, etc. Without a Live ID account you would be losing out on the ultimate Windows Phone experience that everyone has been raving about.

One of the first things you need to choose when signing up for a Live ID account is your email address. You can use an existing email address with a different service (such as Gmail, Yahoo or AOL), but if you do, you will not be able to store your calendar with your Live ID as a backup. In this case, just create a new one and use it as your backup. Windows Phone has no limitations on how many email/calendar/contact accounts you can add to your smartphone, so we will also go through the steps of adding more accounts in another chapter.

This Live ID information is critical to ensuring that you get the best experience on your Windows Phone, so I strongly suggest that you provide the most accurate information you can. Your Live ID account will be used to setup your other services and will be used to channel your contacts, calendar and other services including social networks that may be Microsoft-based or third parties such as Facebook, Flickr, YouTube, LinkedIn, MySpace, SmugMug, Pandora, Picasa, etc.

Import Contacts, Calendar and Appointments

Now that you have your Live ID credentials and you have your contacts from your old phone in a file, you can start adding them into your contacts section in your Live account. Please note that there are ways to import those contacts by simply providing a file and avoiding to type all those contacts. You Live ID account allows you to import contacts from many different sources such as Microsoft Outlook, Facebook, AOL, MySpace, etc.

If you don't want to mess with imports and files or you don't have your contacts in any of these services, you can still go "old school" and type them one by one. Type as much information you have about them, this will come in handy once you activate your Windows Phone and start connecting to other services. Even if you imported your contacts, you may still want to complete or complement that information with as much as you can because it can be used to match your contacts across multiple social media services such as Facebook, Twitter, etc.

Let's say you have a contact for John Doe, (555) 123-4567 in your old phone, but you also know that John's email address is JDoe@hotmail.com. You can enter the email address when you are creating the contact by typing it in. Let's just say that John also has a LinkedIn account that you are linked with and that he also has a Facebook account with that same email address. Then, John's Facebook wall and LinkedIn profile updates will appear on your phone right after you setup your Facebook and LinkedIn to your Windows Phone. Even more, when John calls you, you will see his latest Picture from Facebook or LinkedIn (whichever he updated last), without having done anything at all! Additionally, you will be able to "link" all the entries from John and make them appear as a single entry.

Calendar and Appointments are an easy import into Live services if you have Outlook, if not, I will recommend you to get those appointments into Outlook and then from there you can have Live services import from your Outlook. The same "old school" principle applies, if you don't feel secure with imports and files, then you can just type those entries into your Live ID account.

For importing from your current PIM (personal information manager) contact information into your Live ID account, you can go to http://profile.live.com/connect At the time of writing this book, Live services offered to import information from Facebook, MySpace, LinkedIn, AOL Mail, Hyves, Gmail, Hi5, Tagged, Microsoft Outlook and another Windows Live account. These services may change as time goes by and more or less options may be offered.

Configure Windows Live Services

If you have not logged into you profile, you may need some updating on that page. This is the demographic information I mentioned before. You can access that page directly by going to http://profile.live.com

Once in your profile, you can edit what you want others to see and how much information is visible to the outside world. You can choose to share your personal details with everyone, friends of friends, friends only or nobody at all. How public you make your profile is a personal matter that is your choice alone. Your experience will not be hindered by choosing a more private setting. I normally am careful about who I setup as friends so I leave my choices open to my friends, but some settings still private.

One thing nice on your Live ID account is that you can change your status from your profile page, your Messenger app, your Windows Phone and other apps. Your status is a short text you can enter right after your name. For example; while I was writing this book I kept my friends updated by setting my status to "Second chapter of my book is done!"; another way you can use it is with some Windows applications such as Windows Media Player or Last.fm to change your status as it applies to that particular application by broadcasting out what music you are listening to.

Additionally you can link your Live ID account to the services you are interested in, such as Hulu, Picasa, Flickr, WordPress and many other services. This is where you can choose from the services you frequently use on your computer. Live will find commonalities between your different accounts (Live, Facebook, LinkedIn, Twitter and email) and these services you choose from. For example matching your John Doe's email address having a match to a login in Picasa, so that when you are on your Windows Phone, you can see under Pictures >> What's New or under People >> What's New all the picture feeds from John's Picasa account.

It's these little connections what makes your Windows Phone truly yours. This is what let's your phone become a window to your own life and your friend's lives without having to deal in the process with a million different usernames and passwords.

Email Setup

This book will help you setup your email accounts in your Windows Phone, but in this section we are only preparing the field. As long as you know that your email accounts all work without problems outside of your phone, all you need to prepare is your account information (email address, password, email server settings, etc.) If you just created a new Live ID account, you might as well test your new email address by sending a few emails either to your other email account or someone that can reply whether they successfully received the email or not.

If you already have an email account (or several email accounts, like I do) I will suggest you to create one that uses a Live ID account (Hotmail.com or Live.com). You should not completely replace your existing email accounts with this new one (although you could if you wanted to), and you can setup as many email accounts as you want. The idea of using a Live ID account and its corresponding email address is that your services will tie to this account as we will see in other sections of this book. You experience with Windows Phone will be so much better with a Live ID account that I cannot stress this enough.

If you are concerned that your current email account(s) may or may not be supported, please don't. Windows Phone can connect with multiple different methods to different types of email servers. As a general rule, if you can connect to your email account with Microsoft Outlook, Windows Live Mail (also known as Microsoft Outlook Express) or you use an online email provider (such as Gmail, Yahoo, AOL, etc.); then your email account is definitely supported. After using Windows Phones for over 2 years, I have not found a single user who was not able to connect to their email account with Windows Phone.

Xbox LIVE and Zune Services

Xbox LIVE and Zune services are the exclusive media offering that Microsoft has for all Windows Phones.

Preparing the field for these services will include the following steps: creating an Xbox LIVE account on Xbox.com if you don't already have one, installing Zune Software on your Windows PC, and creating a new profile in Zune Software if you have not done so yet. Please note that these two services may not be enabled in your country yet (many countries are supported and the list keeps growing weekly). Don't despair, if you live outside the supported countries, you can still install the Zune Software and use it for syncing with your Windows Phone, listening to your music, and watching your videos and movies. As a general rule, I would say that if you were able to purchase a Windows Phone in your country and you cannot use these services, then you are most likely going to be able to start using them really soon. Microsoft is making all efforts to expand their user base into as many countries as possible. Your absolutely worst case scenario is that you may not be able to purchase music and video offerings through these services if they are not provided in your country. Microsoft's goal is to be able to offer these services worldwide, regardless of the country. The legal requirements for selling copyrighted media across countries are so different that it may take Microsoft a bit longer to get to your location.

For either accounts, the setup process is very simple: by now you already have a Live ID account, which will be the way these websites will identify you. Simply go to the websites mentioned below and you will be able to create the profile after providing your Live ID credentials. The information that can carry over from your Live ID profile is carried automatically to your profile on both of these services so you have to type less.

You can play Xbox LIVE games and use your Xbox LIVE account that you normally use to play on your Xbox (if you have one, but you don't need one). The Xbox LIVE service can be used to get games that add "gamer score" that can be used to brag to your friends how well you did on some games, or to simply pair you up with other gamers and compare your scores to theirs. Some games use your current score stored in your Xbox LIVE account to match you to the other gamers that have a similar score so neither player has an unfair advantage and the game is both more enjoyable and challenging for both players. The new Xbox Metro UI, released in November of 2011 for your Xbox gaming system allows your Windows Phone to control some games from the smartphone or get more information into your Windows Phone about what you are watching or playing on your Xbox 360 or even use your Windows Phone as a remote control for your Xbox game system's media functions. Not all games on your Windows Phone are prepared to interact with the Xbox LIVE service or your Xbox 360, but the ones that do, add a whole new dimension to gaming on your console, PC and smartphone as we currently know them.

You can also take advantage from your Zune account for music, videos, TV shows and movies from your Windows Phone. The Zune account is the service that you would use to access unlimited music and video streaming (for a monthly access fee) or you would use to purchase individual songs, videos, TV shows and movies. The unlimited access is called Zune Pass and it gives you unlimited music video streaming to any of their more than 14 million songs among other for a nominal monthly fee. You can still get the Zune service account for free and only use their basic services. Once you have the free service, you can also use it for "renting" videos, TV shows and movies where you pay a lower fee than purchasing but you have a limited amount of time to view the video. In this case you only pay for what you choose to rent and purchase, there is no monthly commitment of any kind. As an example, you can rent a movie for 14 days until you watch it, and then you can keep it for 24 hours after the first play. The great thing about this method is that it is obviously less expensive than purchasing a movie and you are not immediately required to watch the video. One of the coolest features is that you can rent a movie, start watching it on your smartphone, continue on your PC and complete watching it on your Xbox 360 (in the Zune service that comes bundled in your Xbox 360).

Installing the Zune Software is easy and takes a few minutes. The software is a free download from Microsoft (you can also get it at Zune.com). The Zune Software will not only allow you to purchase, download and watch media on your PC, but it is also used to send those media files to your Windows Phone and other supported media devices. Additionally, you will have to use your Zune Software for some of the Windows Phone OS updates that are larger than usual.

The update process includes a backup before every update is performed to make sure that you can roll back to your backed up setup if you find any problems while attempting an upgrade. At this time I have been through 5 different updates on each of the Windows Phones I have and have not had any problems... With the updates to the Zune Software, the update process is even more refined than the previous ones. Zune Software checks for updates (much like your Windows PC does) at the moment you connect your Windows Phone to your PC via a USB cable (or when you sync via Wi-Fi). If it does find an update, it will prompt you if you want to run an update or not. If you answer "Yes", then you basically leave your Windows Phone working (make sure it has enough power if you are updating over Wi-Fi, or it is plugged in to your PC via USB). After a few minutes, backup and smartphone reboots; you get an updated smartphone with the newest features enabled (all by simply pressing one button on your desktop). Please note that some updates help take advantage of newer hardware features. For example, you will not be able to use the features that become active with a front-facing camera, increased megapixel counts on your camera or get 4G broadband speed unless you have the device with the appropriate hardware to take advantage of these enhancements in the OS.

What Kind Of Accounts Will I Be Able To Setup On My Windows Phone?

As I mentioned earlier, accounts are not just for email. There are a myriad of services available online that Windows Phone OS can take advantage of. While you may not want to invest yourself in an all Microsoft move, you certainly can use all the connections offered by your Live ID account, and your already existing accounts for the online services and social networks you already use on your Windows PC. Windows Phone OS supports you connecting to a single Live ID account, mainly because this information is available throughout the smartphone for validating the services we already discussed. If you created a second Live ID account, you will not be able to connect to other than email, calendar and contacts. Your other apps will still use your main Live ID (the one you setup on the initial setup).

Accounts can be setup for Windows Live ID, Outlook/Exchange, Office 365, Yahoo! Mail, Google/Gmail, etc. AT&T offers a service named AT&T Address Book that keeps a copy of your contacts (that may come in from other phones that are not smartphones). This may be the way you can resolve accessing your already existing contact in your old phone. The other carriers have a similar way to handle your contacts, so this applies also to them. Generic account setup connections are provided for POP and IMAP where you job may offer access via these protocols. These protocols are older and do not provide much support for push notifications and push email. Push emails are sent to your smartphone as opposed to having your smartphone connect on a schedule (say, every 15 minutes, or every hour). POP and IMAP connections require that your phone dial into the email server at a given interval whether there are emails waiting for you or not. The down side of using these protocols is that you don't get the email at the exact time it was sent, and you end up using more data because your phone has to keep connecting to the server to see if there is anything out there waiting for you to download. Additionally, you can also add accounts for Facebook, Twitter and LinkedIn to create a more personalized experience.

On a more technical note, some Email servers that were not created by Microsoft, use Exchange ActiveSync (EAS) as a protocol (such as Gmail, Google Apps and many others). So while your specific email service is not named in this list, it is still supported. In fact Gmail and Google Apps accounts can be setup both as Google accounts and Exchange accounts because they use this compatible protocol. As a fallback process all email services offer either POP or IMAP services, have this in mind in case you have problems connecting to your email server, but before setting up your account as POP or IMAP, ask your email administrator (or tech support) what is the email server or email protocol used in your case. They will be able to provide you the information you need to connect into your work email service.

Chapter 3: Choose The Best Phone For You

At this point you have already prepared the field outside of your smartphone. You updated all your Live settings, brought it up to the point where you can go out and search for the latest and greatest. There are some really good options out there... you can go with the most recent smartphones released which have high speed processors, front and back cameras (the front one for video calling, the one in the back for taking pictures – coming in up to 8 megapixels) or you may decide not to break your budget and go with last year's smartphones which by now are all confirmed as update-able to the newest Windows Phone OS offering. Even if you go with the current "flagship Windows Phone" (the most advanced and feature-rich device at the time); your price range will be somewhere between FREE and $200 provided you sign up for a one or two year service contract. Microsoft has announced some offerings for new smartphone users where they will be able to get the latest OS features at entry-point prices while still getting really great products.

One of the situations that Microsoft has suffered from in the past, particularly with older mobile OS's was to allow mobile manufacturers make all the calls when it came to choosing the hardware that would be included in these mobile devices. While this may have sounded great to ensure enough options to choose from in the market; it ended up creating more problems than it resolved. Some manufacturers made great hardware, this reason alone was great, but then again Microsoft did not prevent manufacturers from modifying the UI, so over time, the best hardware ended up having a UI that did not resemble at all the software that was actually running behind the scenes. Microsoft slowly lost control of its own platform leading to some good UI ideas but mostly bad, slow and flaky implementations of a user interface that did nothing for most users. Some manufacturers even ended up choosing hardware that barely performed with the requirements but did not meet the users' expectations. In some cases, there was faulty or low quality hardware as well as faulty device drivers. In the end, this practice hurt the manufacturers that ended up not selling as many units as they wanted and it hurt Microsoft badly causing bad PR. Windows Mobile PDAs were great, but when the market opened up for smartphones the quality ended up declining because it was such a low margin market. Some products were still incredible and had wide user adoption, but in general it was a time of high market fragmentation into whatever the manufacturers wanted to do with the OS. A similar case is happening today with Google's Android OS. Google is however, trying to keep manufacturers somewhat under control by releasing "Nexus flagship products" in agreement with some of the manufacturers. This way, other competing manufacturers need to compete with the flagship products with equivalent features.

This time around, Microsoft took the bull by the horns and decided to publish a more detailed and controlled set of hardware specifications for the manufacturers to choose from. The hardware specifications are very detailed at listing the minimum parameters at which the hardware needs to perform. This means that the specifications include great hardware; they are advanced enough and expected to hit a sweet spot between performance and price that leaves consumers pleasantly surprised while getting a consistent experience when using all the different smartphones that run Windows Phone. The consumer benefits the most, you don't need to learn a new UI if you go from HTC to Samsung to Nokia. It's all Windows Phone OS, it should and it does feel the same; all consistent, all tailored to you. Some, if not most of the device drivers were built in-house. At the same time, the specs leave enough room for the manufacturers to create a series of devices that are uniquely attractive to consumers while performing amazingly well and keeping the user experience consistent across the board.

The typical variance between Windows Phones centers around two main components: screen size and keyboard. While all screens are 800 x 480 pixels, there are devices with screens between 3.5 inches (diagonally) and 4.7 inches. Some screens are regular LCDs, others are AMOLED and some even Super AMOLED which have extremely vibrant colors and use less battery than others. Some Windows Phones come with the screen built on Gorilla Glass. Gorilla Glass is a technology by Corning that comprises a specially formulated glass layering system that ensures better screen image quality, even in direct sunlight plus better resistance to scratches and breakage. The other point of differentiation between Windows Phones is the keyboard; here there are smartphones with and without keyboards. The ones that do not have a keyboard rely on the on-screen keyboard for all input and have a thinner and lighter design. The ones that do have a physical keyboard have a slide-out keyboard that is either portrait or landscape (vertical or horizontal slide-out). These offer a variety of key sizes and tactile feedback. Another differentiating hardware feature on Windows Phones is speakers; HTC manufactures slide-out stereo speakers in one of its Windows Phones. This smartphone (HTC Surround) delivers rich sound in Dolby mobile or SRS WOW HD is aimed at the media focused consumer. Some Windows Phones even come with memory expansion slots.

The Samsung Focus for example can be expanded up to an additional 32 gigabytes bringing it to 40 GB total. However the expansion is not handled as it is on other smartphones, when memory is added to a Windows Phone, it needs to be "integrated" and after that, it becomes a part of the smartphone completely integrated with the internal memory. Therefore, removing it will require that you reset and bring your phone back to the manufacturer's original settings, requiring you to install your apps all over again.

All Windows Phones come with a processor of at least single-core 1 GHz processing speed and 5 MP (mega pixel) picture cameras that can also shoot 720p HD video. They all offer a great music listening experience and some like the Nokia Lumia 720, 800, 900, the Samsung Focus (or the Samsung Omnia 7) offer excellent picture quality as cameras. The minimum amount of memory provided for installing apps, storing music and videos is 8 GB (gigabytes). Microsoft has been so extremely detailed the hardware specifications that they even required that these smartphones should have a picture/shutter button. You may think that this is a detail that is not as important as one may think, but this allows Microsoft to rely on this button being pressed right out of your pocket to take a quick picture even when it was locked. Think about it, if the button was not there, you would have to take the smartphone out of your pocket, turn it on, search for the camera app, tap on it and then take the picture. By the time you ended following all these steps, your picture opportunity is already gone.

This attention to detail added to the hard work they have done on the software side has earned Microsoft back the consumer trust they enjoyed in the past and the praise and awards in the consumer design arena.

Windows Phone devices have been out in the market since November 2010. Microsoft has committed to upgrade ALL smartphones they released with Windows Phone OS v7 to Windows Phone OS v7.5. The meaning of this is very significant because at this point, it means that there are Windows Phones that are about 1 year old and extremely affordable that can enjoy the newest features that the brand new phones enjoy. You can find Windows Phones for as little as $0.01 or even free at online retailers such as Amazon.com and from time to time at the carrier stores. In this particular case, a big difference with Android smartphones is that because the manufacturers keep renewing their offering, it is hard to find Android smartphones for a competitive price other than when the retailers want to get rid of their acquired stock.

In November of 2011 a new generation of Windows Phone smartphones was already out and with that, the new agreement that Microsoft signed with Nokia came to fruition when two smartphones were released. Nokia released the Nokia Lumia 710 and the Nokia Lumia 800. The Lumia 700 series being the "low end" still offers great features considered equal or better than 2010's smartphones from their competitors. The Lumia 800 has an incredible look and is smaller, faster, better than almost any other Windows Phone smartphone out there. The AMOLED screens of both smartphones are a decent size, extremely bright and colorful. In early 2012, Nokia expanded its offering with the Lumia 600 series; a low end Windows Phone and the Lumia 900 which uses 4G wireless broadband.

Please note that Windows Phones will be slightly different and while the particular offerings on each country will have some differences; you can be certain that the overall experience will be the same and the hardware will be essentially the same.

That pushy sales guy

We've all been there; you get to the store after having analyzed which carrier is more convenient for you. You can base it all on contract length, maximum bandwidth in your area (usually not as good as advertised), or simply because they carry the phone you are interested in purchasing. Normally, it doesn't matter what your reason is... even though you explained the sales guy what you were looking for. The sales guy will offer you the phone that will give him the largest profit margin he can get. Make sure to stay focused and do not let the sales rep distract you from the process of getting what you want.

Microsoft ran into an unforeseen situation with sales reps all across the country where they had the option of offering Android OS, BlackBerry OS and Windows Phone OS powered phones; where they were pushing Android OS phones simply because they would leave them a higher profit margin. Studies have proven that users who test drive Windows Phone OS will end up buying the device simply because "they get it". It is simple, intuitive and it creates a phone that is uniquely personalized just by signing into the services mentioned before in this book.

Additionally, some of those sales reps didn't even know the difference between Windows Phone OS devices and assumed that they were just the newer versions of the old Windows Mobile, and that they would simply carry on with the issues of fragmentation and unstable platform. Unfortunately we are not just talking about a few "rotten apples", but quite a large percentage of the wireless sales force did not even bother reading (or even testing) the new product line from Microsoft. I have made it a personal goal to visit several different wireless carriers asking around and seeing what their sales reps would say. When they did not agree with reality I would quite simply pull my Windows Phone and perform a quick 5 minute demo. Showing them how far this personalization would go and how easy it would be to do so. Most of the sales reps I "educated" myself changed their attitude towards this platform and whenever appropriate, they recommend the proper platform.

Of course, none of these issues would happen if all sales reps were knowledgeable in the products they sell, or even if they at least read the documentation they need to read before calling themselves sales reps... just remember you are the consumer and if you don't like being rushed or pressured into purchasing a smartphone you are not sure about, you can always walk out and go to another store.

Although I would be excited if everyone would instantly understand, like and purchase Windows Phones; I am not saying you should not look and shop around. This is a commitment that you will make with your wireless carrier for the next 20-24 months: OK, OK, some of us change our cell phones on a shorter cycle, I admit it. In any case, you should not make a rushed decision. I have been pleasantly surprised with Windows Phone users that after a year of having the same smartphone, they still love their device and don't feel the rush into purchasing a new device.

Chapter 4: Initial Setup - A Step By Step Guide

Now that you purchased a new Windows Phone smartphone, we need to get it out of the box and going. If you are like me, then you probably cannot wait for the smartphone to charge completely. Don't worry; most smartphones come with at least a half battery's worth of power. You will be able to set it up (if you want) while you are giving it its first charge. You might get lucky and power it up to find a full battery. Great for you!

Let's get started.

Protect Your Windows Phone

At a minimum, you are getting the smartphone, a battery, a charger and headset (hard or in-ear-soft ear buds). Some carriers are throwing in also additional items such as a screen protector film and/or a case.

Film protectors are those sticky plastic pieces that are trimmed to the size and shape of your smartphone's screen that protect the screen from getting scratches and dents. If your smartphone falls, you are also somewhat protected against cracking. Screen protectors come in several different types, some are harder plastic and others seem to be made of a soft substance that offers better protection. Cases are used to protect the whole phone from scratches or total breakage in case of a fall. Cases are made of either hard or soft materials such as leather, faux leather, plastic or silicone. They come in multiple formats, with and without cover for the screen (if you get one with a cover, then you mostly won't need a screen protector). Hard cases made of plastic come in the form of two plates that snap together to cover the sides and back of the smartphone. Cases made of leather are great protection but they mostly add bulk to the phone. If you purchased a smartphone that was thin and light, you should at least see how much bulk a leather case will add because it will and in the end it may not be as "pocketable" as you may have thought to begin with. Most leather cases come with a nub and a belt holder so you may want to keep it handy off your belt. Silicone cases are the most common since they are typically thin, don't add much bulk to the overall size of the phone and still give it an all-around protection against falls.

If your smartphone did not come bundled with any of these, I strongly recommend that you protect it by getting them from somewhere like Amazon.com where they have a huge selection of types and colors. For screen protectors I suggest that you buy Zagg Invisible Shield for the screen. These protectors are great and can stand a real beating from keys and other sharp objects. For cases you can go to a website like Amazon.com and purchase one but make sure it is exactly for your smartphone's brand and model so that it fits well and it does not come loose over time.

Initial Setup

This is a surprisingly simple process. Mainly because by now you did most of the work online and your phone will sync-up with your web services and get that information.

In any case, the process is extremely easy and it takes no more than a few screens. At the very least, you need to select the language in which you want to setup Windows Phone. You move to the next screen by touching the "next" button. Then comes the terms of use where you can read the conditions under which you are licensed to use the device. There is really no option here… if you were not to agree to use under these terms you basically cannot use the smartphone, so touch on next. Then you have an option to select whether you want to setup Windows Phone in "recommended" or "custom" form. This is where you choose whether to send usage information to Microsoft so they can learn from your experience or not. Then comes the time-zone selection screen, the device will already come with your current time-zone selected, as it picks up that information from the cellular network where it is running. Then you select whether to sign in with your Windows Live ID (or Passport) credentials we used before to setup your online services. Entering them right now will help you finish the setup faster and not have to do it later. As I mentioned it before, with these credentials you will be able to sync with all your online services we setup earlier and also to use the Zune music, Xbox LIVE and Marketplace services to download music, games and apps respectively.

Once you enter all this information you can touch the "Sign In" button. Please note that at any time during this process you can also touch the "previous" button to go back to the previous screen and make any corrections you may want to do.

Signing in will show a small animation of a few dots rushing across the screen; this means that the phone is communicating with the server to validate the credentials you entered before. A few moments later you will be greeted with an "All Done" screen where you need to touch the "done" button to get to your Windows Phone Home Screen.

You're set!

At this point you can use your phone as a regular phone and you will notice that some of the tiles are moving. You will see that your contacts are not there just yet. It will take a few moments to download them from your online services, but if you are patient, you will see that they will start appearing.

I See Text And Objects On The Screen But What Do They Mean?

Just as Windows Phone OS is easy to learn, it is also like nothing you have ever seen before. Your Windows Phone screens can be:

- Tile collections (i.e. your Home Screen): Each square (or tile) represents a "shortcut" into your app or a particular section within your app. Tiles can refresh with information coming from within the app trying to tell you what's going on. For example; the people tile refreshes with pictures from your contacts from all your social sites and your Live account, the Calendar tile shows you your next appointment in addition. If you "pin" someone's contact to your Home Screen; for example your best friend, your spouse, your kids you will see by default their contact picture take the whole tile, but as soon as they update their social networks' status; you will see their post or their new picture, and if they sent you a text message or you missed a call from them you will see that information refresh on the tile until you read the information or call them back.
- Hubs: Think of these as "screens that cannot fit in one screen". Let's take the people hub as an example. When you touch the People tile, you go into the People Hub. This is an app that has multiple pivots, screens or pages that seem

to be tied one next to the other, so if you swipe with your finger from left to right or right to left you will cycle through all pages. These pages are officially called "Pivots". I will call them "hub pages" or "pivot pages" or simply "Pages" in this book. Some hubs have more pages than others. You can go from one to the other and after the last one you will come back to the first page where you landed. Back to the People Hub: you will find a title at the top of your screen (in this case "people") that spans multiple pages (letting you know you can swipe to the right). The subtitle tells you what that particular pivot page contains. The People Hub contains "recent" (which spans two screens) with tiles of the people you called recently, "all" with a list of all your contacts where you can do a quick search by using the magnifying glass button, then you have a "what's new" page that quickly pulls from your broadband connection (or your Wi-Fi connection) the most recent status, pictures and comments from your social networks.

- Forms: In the end you still have to enter information, select from different options, enter passwords, etc. Forms are very similar to forms on other OSs (including Windows). There are some very minor differences, but you can find these extremely similar across the different platforms (even mobile platforms). You will find labels to show the title of a field. Text-boxes for you to enter text. Checkboxes (which allow for selecting or de-selecting options). Clusters of radio buttons of which you can only select a single option and the others are de-selected. Selection lists (see below) for selecting one option out of a list. Finally you will also see buttons which in Windows Phone OS can take two basic shapes: rectangles and circles. Rectangular buttons are used for showing text describing the action that the button will do when you touch it. Round buttons show only an icon representing the action the button will execute when touched. Some icon buttons are displayed at the bottom of the screen with a "..." on the right corner of the bottom bar. This means you can touch the "..." to expand. In this case you will see a word describing the round buttons right underneath plus you may see a list of additional actions you can take. This list of additional actions is scrollable up and down by swiping.

- Selection Lists: The Metro UI used in Windows Phone OS does not have drop down lists. When you select an object that contains a list from which to select, the whole screen is used to list your options and scroll up and down. Once you select an option, the screen returns to the form where you came from originally.

These are most of the conventions that Metro apps will use. Apps will mostly conform to the Metro UI design principles. The apps that are usually outside of it are games; but they have their own set of conventions they usually apply to.

When you go into an app, you will be able to close it by touching either the "back" hardware button which will close the current page and take you back to the previous page (until you exit the app). Closing it and unloading it from memory, taking you where you were before opening the app. You can also touch the "Windows" hardware button that takes you back to the Home Screen but it leaves the app running in the background. For example, you are writing a text message to someone and you remember you need to enter an appointment. Touch the Windows button go to Calendar, enter a new appointment and when you are done, you can touch the back button until you get to the Messaging app or touch Windows to go to the Home Screen and then touch the Messaging tile to go back into the Messaging app. You can press "Back" for an extended time (about two seconds) and you will be able to see the apps that are currently running. Slide sideways to see all apps and touch the one you want to switch into and you will jump right into it.

Keyboard conventions: At any time, when you touch a control that allows you to enter text, the keyboard will appear. If the field you touch allows only for numbers, then a numeric keypad will appear. Sometimes apps will allow for the full keyboard but they intend for you to enter numeric values only. On my first day with my Windows Phone I was pleasantly surprised about how responsive and effective the soft keyboard really was. They full keyboard has several "modes". The default is the one that shows you a QUERTY keyboard. You can enter lower and upper case characters, there is a backspace, comma, space and period keys in addition to an "enter" key. On the lower left corner of your keyboard you will find that there is a key labeled "&123". This key changes mode to numeric and symbol keyboard. There are two types of numeric and symbol keyboards. Both of them show the number keys on top plus they show all symbols allowed. Each of the two numeric and symbol keyboards are accessed by touching a right and left arrow key right over the "abcd" key which is used to go back to the regular QUERTY keyboard.

Sometimes, when the scenario allows it, you may see a smiley face symbol. This key enables the several emoticon symbol keyboards that you can use in apps like messaging and chatting.

Let's See What You Have So Far On Your Smartphone:

Different Windows Phones will look somewhat different on the outside, but the inside is fairly similar. The main differences will be given by the owner's data (what makes your smartphone yours) and the different apps you may download and have ready to be used. By the same token, carriers and manufacturers can add a degree of customization but it is very limited. The limitations are rigid, but as I mentioned it before, they are to benefit the user with a consistent user experience. This leaves custom apps that both the carriers and manufacturers may want to make available to the user. Different vendors will provide you with more or less custom apps.

I will focus on the standard experience you will have on any Windows Phone, the specific apps bundled from the carriers and manufacturers can be removed or re-downloaded so they are for all intents and purposes just like free apps you can install.

You Home Screen will have the following tiles:

- Phone is the app that lets you make calls, see your call history, access you voicemail, and go into your contact list.
- People: this is your contact list, not just your contact list for making calls but the list of all your contacts in your social networks, you can see the status from each and every one of them in real time just as you can add information about each of them if you want to. This tool can also be used to search a contact, and then selecting the way to contact them. For example you can search for John; once found, you will be offered a list of contact addresses: call mobile phone, text him, email him, IM him or char via Facebook chat with him. Selecting each of these options will jump to the appropriate app to complete that task.
- Messaging: This is the app that lets you send text messages (via SMS messaging); connect into Facebook chat, Live Messenger, etc. This tool knows whether your contacts are available over Facebook chat or IM, allowing you to contact them via those channels instead of using up a text message. If you don't

have unlimited text messages, this is a great way to save you from potential overages.

- Email: Opens the email app which defaults into your inbox, you can use this app to review any emails that you have available online.

One or two rows of tiles may appear here, they are optional and specific to each carrier so they can add whatever apps they choose to use here. These are custom apps that can be removed from the Home Screen, uninstalled and re-installed for free from the Marketplace from the section that is specific to the carrier or the manufacturer.

- Calendar: This is another of the basic features found on Windows Phones that allow you to sync your appointments to your Live account. Keep your tasks here as well. Your Calendar Hub lets you see your appointments in day or agenda modes. You can also see your "to-do" items in another pivot page.
- Internet Explorer: A lot has been said about your web browser on mobile platforms. The implementation of Internet Explorer in Windows Phone screams performance. It is equivalent to Internet Explorer 9 on your desktop and it outperforms most of the other mobile platform browsers, even while the OS is running on a single-core processor.
- Xbox LIVE/Games: This is your games hub. There are Xbox LIVE games and regular games. Xbox LIVE games allow you to interact with your Xbox 360, report on your achievements for comparing, bragging or competing online with your buddies. Regular games are games that do not report your achievements and don't interact with your Xbox LIVE account; they are also listed in this hub.
- Pictures: This is yet another hub with great functionality. Your first page in the Pictures Hub has several links that can take you to your Camera Roll: where all the pictures you take with your phone are stored. Albums: where pictures are grouped by category, for example your picture collections in Facebook if you have them grouped. Date: where the pictures are ordered by date. People: where you see the pictures grouped by contact. You can choose what contact you want to get their pictures and it automatically updates them when you go into that tile. The Favorites page in the pictures hub is a way to add some pictures that will become the background of your pictures hub. Use the "…" button for that. There is also a "What's New" pivot page that gets all the

pictures from your contacts and shows them in reverse chronological order here.

- Music + Videos: This is your "media hub" where you can find all your media files, music, videos podcasts, radio (yes, you can do regular FM radio on your device) and access to the marketplace to purchase more music. The hub is divided into a Zune page where you access the items I mentioned above; a History page that shows what media you played recently; a New page that shows the recently acquired media files (such as podcasts, video or music) that you may have downloaded from your PC recently; the Apps page shows apps you have on your device that make use of your media files. Any music streaming (such as Last.fm, Slacker, etc.) would show up here along with some Video apps such as YouTube app.

- Marketplace: This is the hub where you download free and paid content and apps. The Marketplace Hub is divided into several pages: The main page contains a short list of the categories you can go into, where each category is a hub in itself. The Apps page shows a few featured apps and a link into a list of all apps which takes you to the Apps hub. "Games" behaves in the same way where you have a few games featured and a link to go into the games hub of the Marketplace. The Music page also behaves in the same way where a few artists are listed and you can go to the music hub by touching the all music link. Finally, there is one more page that shows the latest featured item out of the whole marketplace. This item can be an artist (with a link to their latest release), an app or a game. This item rotates every few hours giving you the ability to see what is out there without getting too deep into the hub's options. At all times, you can touch the search icon-button and search for that particular type of media (music, podcast, apps, games, etc.) Additionally your smartphone carrier and manufacturer get to have their exclusive hub here where you can access apps from each of them designed for their products. Your bundled software from them can be found in these hubs.

- Office: Windows Phone is the only smartphone with access to Microsoft Office. Other platforms may have apps that are more or less compatible with Office, but they are not the real deal. If you normally use Office apps on your PC, you may want to take a look at the features offered by Windows Phone OS. You can edit MS Word, MS Excel, MS PowerPoint, MS OneNote, MS SharePoint, etc. You can even access information stored in a number of different locations, such as your smartphone (obviously), SkyDrive, MS Office 365; Microsoft's cloud offering for office productivity and SharePoint when used as a repository of Office files.

- Me: The "me" tile may seem somewhat redundant. Why would someone want to have a tile about them? The answer is quite simple. This is the hub that tells you all that is happening around you on the web. Once you open this tile, you land on the Profile page, here you can see and change your status to all your social networks and chat apps. In the Notifications page you can see any new notifications that were sent to you from your social networks. Some people prefer to contact you in different ways, some will call you, some will try to chat with you and others will just post to your wall on Facebook, here is where you see a list of all that Facebook is receiving in your name on your wall or as a reply to a comment you may have made on someone else's comment. These items are also listed in your tile's animation in the Home Screen. The "What's New" page also lists the feeds from your social networks and IM grouped by comment thread.

You may see other tiles show up in the Home screen of your Windows Phone, some may be specific to the manufacturer and others may be from your carrier. In any case all tiles can also be accessed in the apps list. All the apps in your smartphone will be listed here, whether they were bundled in your phone or downloaded/purchased from the marketplace app. You can access the apps list by touching the round button with an arrow to the right (or swiping with your finger on the screen from right to left).

A list grouped and ordered alphabetically will be displayed; you can scroll by swiping your finger on the screen up and down. Swiping from left to right will take you back to the Home Page (the same as touching the Windows button on your phone). If you touch one of the letters you will be taken to a list of all letters and you will be able to quick jump to that letter in the list. Letters that have no applications are disabled. When at the top of the app list, you will also see two buttons one with an arrow to go back to the home screen and another with a magnifying glass. This is the "search" button. The search button in the app list lets you search for a specific app. Just start typing the name of the app you are looking for and you will see how the list starts showing the items that match your search criteria.

Your smartphone is not just a collection of a dozen tiles or so... Your Windows Phone includes an impressive amount of apps right off the box. These "basic apps" are what most beginners will need, save some games and maybe a few particular app or so you may be interested in downloading and installing.

Let's focus on the basic apps in your Windows Phone, these are:

- Alarms: Let's you setup a number of alarms with the ability to choose what ringtone to use. You can set up alarms to ring at a particular time, on specific days of the week. You can name each of these alarms so you can quickly identify them. Most Windows Phones are loud enough to be used as alarm clocks. I personally use it every day, by leaving a charger in my bedroom and have it wake me up. The alarm sound starts off at a low volume and keeps going up until it reaches the maximum volume. If you are a heavy sleeper, you can setup multiple alarms, each with a different sound to different times, so you know that you will be awaken.

- Calculator: This is the typical calculator tool. Not much can be said about a typical calculator, but Microsoft has added a pretty nifty trick you can do with it. Hold your smartphone in portrait mode and you will have a standard calculator. Hold your smartphone in landscape mode and the calculator rotates and turns into a scientific calculator.

- Calendar: This is a hub that contains your daily scheduled activities from all your accounts. Those accounts can be any of the supported types such as Hotmail/Live, MS Outlook, MS Exchange, Gmail/Google Apps, etc. The pivot pages are: "Day" which lists the hours in the day and places the appointments in their corresponding hours (using a different color for each calendar, you get to choose what color for each calendar). The "Agenda" page in this hub is a summary view of your appointments showing only the actual appointments, their times and how long they were scheduled for. If a location was entered, it is also displayed. Finally, the "To-Do" page is a list of items you have entered in your to-do list. There is more functionality to this hub: for example you can switch to a full month view to quick jumping to a particular day, month and year.

- Camera: Ever since digital camera prices have come down and hardware became good enough to replace the digital point-and-shoot you would otherwise carry with yourself; cameras have been included in smartphones. This time, Microsoft has requested that cameras should be no less than 5 megapixels when included in Windows Phones. Additionally, the specs also require manufacturers to include a "camera" button that can override the lock on your screen. This means that you can go from pocket to picture in one press of a button and since you carry your smartphone with you all the time, this also makes your smartphone the best way to post your pictures to any number of web services making backups a thing of the past. You can setup your smartphone to automatically copy your pictures to Facebook, Live, SkyDrive; even better: you can have your pictures backed up to your Live account automatically. From the camera menu (right after you take the picture) choose whether to post your picture to Facebook. In addition to taking pictures at high resolution, you can choose a number of settings for those pictures, including auto flash, ISO settings, etc. The camera is also able to record video in HD (in at least 720p resolution).

- Games: No matter what your age is, you should not dismiss this app. If you are an avid gamer, you will find yourself using this hub very often. If you are not, give the games hub a review. No matter how you like to have fun, there are plenty of game options and game types. From action packed, to board games, to card games, to brain teasers, etc. In any case, this is the app that will take you to the Games hub. The games hub has multiple pivot pages. Those are the "Collection" page where you have the list of games installed in your Windows Phone. This list is split into two groups; first you have all your Xbox LIVE games (that is the games that connect to the Xbox LIVE services) and then the rest of the games that do not use the Xbox LIVE services. Another games pivot page is Xbox LIVE; this page shows your "gamertag" with your achievements, Gamerscore, profile and your "digital persona" or "avatar". This page hub also lets you swipe a half page into a group of tiles that shows your "friends", a list of other gamers that you may have friended over time. All these services are free and exclusive to Windows Phone smartphones; if you have an Xbox and use the Xbox LIVE subscription service you can also use messaging between gamers from your Xbox to their Xbox, Xbox to their Windows Phone, from your Windows Phone to their Xbox or from your Windows Phone to their Windows Phone. This is a great way to play across the world against someone that happens to have the same game you do. Some games offer a multiplayer mode, competing live against each other or play turn-by-turn. It solely depends on the game, but this is the framework under which you can challenge someone else to start that game and offer some out-of-game interaction. Any requests for multiplayer game challenges, or turns will be displayed in the "Requests" pivot page. The final pivot page is "Spotlight"; this is where some game promotions are listed. Sometimes you will find great game deals and other times you will find games worth checking out. Most games have a "trial mode" so you can play for a few levels or a limited time trial so you can see if you like the game. If you do, you can purchase it, if you don't, you can just uninstall it. Some games are even free and may or may not show an "ad bar" at the top or bottom of the screen. These ads are what support Windows Phone developers when they choose not to charge users for their apps.

- Internet Explorer: As I mentioned before, this is the web browser included with Windows Phone. This version of IE is equivalent to the desktop version of MS IE 9. You can browse using this IE in both mobile and desktop modes. In mobile mode; most sites will detect you are browsing from a smartphone and serve you a smaller, faster page. You can also choose to browse in desktop mode where you mask your smartphone session as a desktop IE 9 browser session and have the same webpage rendered on your smartphone's screen that you would have on your desktop.

- Maps: This tool is equivalent to going to a mapping website on your desktop computer. The tool takes advantage of your Windows Phone's GPS circuitry and shows you the map of the area where you are located (if you enabled GPS under settings). You get the option of displaying the map in a satellite view or clear map. Clear maps load impressively fast, but satellite view is also fast enough to leave as your default option. Pinch to zoom in or out to see more or less details. Travelling to an unknown area is no longer a problem, with the use of this app and the use of a feature called "Scout". Touch the scout button and you will be taken to a hub that lists nearby entries for "eat + drink", "see + do", "shop" and "highlights". Each of them showing as pushpins on a map on top of the screen. Select one of these pushpins on the map and you will be able to ask for directions from your current location to the selected pushpin. You not only don't need to ask for directions any more, but you now have your own personal scout that knows everything there is to know about the area where you are, even if you don't.

- Marketplace: We touched on this app several times so far, this is a subject that will be recurring throughout this book. Whether you are willing to spend a few dollars for paid apps or you are only interested in using free apps, you will still need to setup your marketplace account. This app is where you search, purchase (even if the price is $0, you still touch the "buy" button), download, install and free update your apps. The service keeps track of the apps you have installed on your device and will let you know whenever there is an update to the app you purchased. On the tile listed in the home screen, you will see a number listed right next to the Marketplace icon, this refers to the number of apps you have in your device that require to be updated. You can choose whether to update or not, but all updates are free of charge, and they normally fix problems that the original app may have had. The Marketplace hub is divided into several hubs, there are two reserved for the carrier and the smartphone manufacturer, the rest of the hubs are divided by category. Once you get to the category itself, you can see a second-level set of hubs that are divided into "top", "free", "new", etc. If you found the app you are looking for, you can tap on that particular app (you are not purchasing it just yet). At this point you are taken to a hub that is dedicated to the app itself where you can see the name of the app, the rating it has (listed in stars out of a 5 star maximum), a general description provided by the developer of the app. The other pages in this app hub are for showing the latest reviews by users of this app (you can write your own review here), screenshots where you can see a few screenshots of the app in question and a "related" pivot page that lists related apps to the current apps. You will find that most competitors of any given app are listed under "related". This is great if you are looking for an app whose name you may not know but you know it is "similar to …" Developers are creating apps and submitting them daily, the total number of apps is growing by the hour. In any case, the growth rate of apps in the Windows Phone Marketplace is actually higher than the app growth rate was in the iPhone's iTunes app store.

- Messaging: The Messaging app lets you communicate with your contacts. You have several communication mediums to do so: SMS/Text Messaging, Facebook chat and Live Messenger chat. The Messaging hub lets you see the Threads pivot page. This page lists all the conversations you had with your contacts via the different ways of communicating you have in this app by listing their name and the date of the last message sent. Once you choose a conversation thread, you are taken to a screen where your messages are listed in detail. Your comments are listed on one side with "conversation bubbles" and your chat contact is listed on the other side with its own set of conversation bubbles. When you chat in this app, you are still bound by the limitations of each medium. For example; text messages are still limited by a number of characters per message. If you go over the limit, then the message gets broken down into several text messages. The other pivot page in this hub is the "Online" page where your contacts are listed by showing their status (their Live Messenger, Facebook chat online status – available, away, etc.) This pivot page only applies to online services as text messages can always be sent and cellular users cannot set a particular "status".

- Music + Videos: This is your smartphone's media hub, called Music + Videos. Again, you are taken to a set of pivot pages where each page corresponds to a category and from there you will be taken to sub-hubs. From the music + videos hub you can go to the Zune page, History, New and Apps. The Zune page has several links that I will detail at the end of this paragraph. The History page shows tiles for the items played most recently. The New page will also show tiles but for the most recent media items received by the device. These media items can be received from the marketplace or synced from your computer via the Zune software. Finally the Apps page will show you some of the apps that exist in your device and are registered as being able to interact with media files that are stored on your device. The Zune page has several links into Music, Videos,

Podcasts, Radio and Marketplace. These are essentially the core of the media experience in your Windows Phone:

- o Music: takes you to your music collection. This implies that you have already synced your Windows Phone and already have your music collection in your device. The options presented to you once you get to this hub will let you search for your music in several different ways.
- o Videos: contains all your videos transferred from your PC. In this hub you will find pages for listing "all videos", TV, music videos, movies and personal videos.
- o Podcasts: If you subscribe to a particular podcast, you will find them here. Detailed lists of your podcasts are listed under two pages: audio and video. The particular podcast settings will determine how many will download to your device at one given time and how long they will remain. If you sync often and normally listen to podcasts, they will keep refreshing every time you sync with your desktop (provided the author releases new podcasts often).
- o Radio: Your smartphone can also receive FM radio signal from your area. As long as you are connected with your headset (it uses the cable as the receiving antenna) you should be able to tune into your local FM stations.
- o Marketplace: will bring you to the marketplace app/hub where you can purchase (or download for free) songs, videos, apps, podcasts, etc.

- Office: This is another exclusive app for Windows Phone smartphones. There may be lots of Microsoft Office look-alikes, but Microsoft Office is exclusively found in smartphones that run Windows Phone OS. Some other platforms have semi-functional versions of Microsoft Office applications (such as OneNote for iOS), but they are not as functional as they are on Windows Phone. The interface of the Office app is in the form of a Hub. The Office Hub is divided into several pages. You will find the "Notes" page that links with OneNote and lists your most recent notes giving you also the ability to access your notebooks that contain all your grouped notes. You will also find the "Documents" page where you can access Excel, Word and PowerPoint documents. The "Locations" page allows you to access your MS Office documents no matter where you are. You will be able to get your documents stored in your smartphone, SkyDrive (linked to your Live account), Office 365; the cloud version of Office that can be found online and SharePoint which is usually used as a document store for some companies. Your company may subscribe to Office 365 or have a SharePoint server, which you may want to take advantage of... Inside each of the applications you will find that they look familiar. Not all the functionality from your regular desktop exists in your smartphone's Excel, Word, OneNote or PowerPoint, but the most useful features are there. You can count on having the ability to open any Office documents with these apps on your Windows Phone.

- People: this is the app that shows you all the information regarding your contacts. It is not called "contacts" simply because that turned out to be too narrow of a name for describing what it does. It is called "People" because it shows you all that is available from the people in your life. Their contact information is a part of it, but it also shows information about the latest that happened to them, their most recent pictures, what's new and so on. All of it gathered from the social networks you have registered on your phone.

- Phone: Phone is the app that lets you make calls, see your call history, access you voicemail, and offers an alternate way to get to the people hub and access your contact list.

- Pictures: This is yet another hub with great functionality. Your first page in the Pictures Hub has several links that can take you to your Camera Roll: where all the pictures you take with your phone are stored. Albums: where pictures are grouped by category, for example your picture albums in Facebook if you have them grouped into different albums. Date: where the pictures are ordered by date. People: where you see the pictures grouped by contact. You can choose what contact you want to get their pictures and it automatically updates them when you go into that tile. The Favorites page in the pictures hub is a way to add some pictures that will become the background of your pictures hub. Use the "..." button for that. There is also a "What's New" pivot page that gets all the pictures from your contacts and shows them in reverse chronological order.

- Settings is the app where you can change the way your smartphone works and behaves. Microsoft was very careful in keeping these settings very simple, having in mind people that are not Power Users. For beginners, I would recommend you not to go into settings unless you want or need to do something in particular (for example connect your Bluetooth device with your smartphone or turn Wi-Fi on/off). If you are willing to explore and go into settings but you are concerned that you might break something, don't be too concerned. Just remember that we just went through the initial setup of your Windows Phone once. It didn't take much time and it was a breeze. Particularly remember that your information is mostly backed up to all those internet services we setup before activating the smartphone. In the highly unlikely and extreme case you were to break something, you can always start over again by resetting to factory settings and starting from scratch (minus the online setup). I will go into detail of the features you can change settings to in a separate chapter.

Chapter 5: A Phone In The Cloud

No, the title for this chapter was not a typo. I didn't mean to say "a phone in the clouds". "The Cloud" as the name of a place is singular. It is used to give a name to the virtual location where your Windows Phone's data is stored. Although "The Cloud" as a term is many things to many people; it is an established convention that it can be used in general as a replacement for "online", where it can mean "a server at vendor X" or "Facebook's 50,000 servers across the globe". The location of each of the server groups does not need to be static. The data that uses this technology is generally speaking sliced, encrypted and spread across multiple locations with fault tolerant processes to ensure data survival in case of a catastrophic data loss in one of the multiple location(s) where it is stored.

What Does It Mean?

We've already seen some glimpses of what this means in this book. You've seen that almost all pieces of the information stored on your phone are also stored online. But you might ask: Is this really safe? The answer is a very assertive YES! Once you understand how this works, you will see this is the case:

So far you have seen that most settings happened online, some services, most of your data, all the information in your phone is inherently backed up or stored online in the internet. But this is not just a matter of saving data in one place, this technique is now called "storage in the cloud" mainly because we have no idea what type of devices are used for this information to be stored, where we are storing this information and even better we cannot see that information unless we are authorized to do so (i.e. by being the users of such devices storing information in the cloud). Not even high level system administrators have access to the actual data in its original unencrypted form. The servers where the information is stored might as well be one or one million servers located in one or one million different "server farms". One of the beauties of this technology is how fault tolerant it is as well as how safe it is. For example when the information is stored in several servers, it is broken down into several pieces, then it is encrypted (to ensure privacy) and then there is additional redundancy to rebuild the original information. To you it just seems that you saved a piece of information... it is a technology that is completely transparent to you. Most people don't even know (or even care) but it is quite amazing how many processes your information goes through to be saved and how quick it is saved (and retrieved from the cloud). Once you need to retrieve it; for example when you replace your Windows Phone with a new one the information is recalled, rebuilt into one piece and sent back to your new device, allowing you to sync back that information. Additionally, because this information is broken down and put back together automatically it also adds another layer of anonymity to each of the bits and pieces stored online. The servers only know that this is piece number 44652 of item 79473056 stored for user number 9458304. Somewhere along the line that information is encrypted so that no one can access raw pieces of that information and attempt to rebuild it and it is only decrypted when it needs to be put back together right before delivering it to your device. Only the system knows how, where and when to rebuild it.

Same As 24/7/365 Backups Without The Hassle

It used to be in the not-so-distant-past, that you would update contact information on your PDA (your personal digital assistant) and you would save it. This information would remain stored in your device until you remembered to sync, backup or copy to another device or your PC. Most people would not backup or sync, which meant that their contacts on their PCs needed to be updated as well. When a device would break or would be lost, you would lose all that valuable information!

Today, you get to save your contact information in your Windows Phone and the information goes straight to your Live account in the cloud. When you get to your PC and open your browser to get to your contacts on that Live account, the information is already there. If you access your live account through MS Outlook or any other client, the information is received and updated automatically. The same thing happens if you are on your computer while you answer the phone and your friend tells you his new home phone: you update it in MS Outlook, it replicates to the cloud and from there to your phone. You only updated it once and it already exists in all your devices. No backups, copies or syncs needed, the cloud does that for you once you registered for all those services.

The end result: you never lose your data. Your effort: almost negligible.

Most of the information in your Windows Phone goes through the same process. The moment you enter it, it almost automatically goes into the cloud. Windows Phone is not the only service that does this, but it has perfected it until it became transparent to the users. Even with older versions of its mobile OS this process was already taking shape and becoming an automated benefit against backups, syncs and copies.

My Windows Phone: More Than A Windows Phone Marketing Site

Microsoft's website address for Windows Phone is http://microsoft.com/windowsphone and it is much more useful than a run of the mill promotional website. This site is a companion to your Windows Phone. Although some of the webpages on it are plain marketing talk, you can find some real use for it! The Windows Phone site is divided into several pages, much like a hub is divided in several main pivot pages! These pages are Discover, Buy, Marketplace, How-To and My Phone. I will not focus too much on the first few pages as they are promotional and intended to direct you to "discover" your phone, where to "buy" a Windows Phone or get to compare Windows Phone devices in order to find the one that better suits you. "Marketplace" is the online version of the Marketplace app in your Windows Phone. You can purchase your apps here from any computer and the apps will be downloaded to your smartphone from the marketplace, no sync required. "How-To" is a very complete set of tutorials on how to use your smartphone with some interesting tips and tricks. Finally, "My Phone" is the section that I would like to go into more detail as it has some interesting functionality to help you take even more advantage of the technology included in your phone.

Click on "My Phone", you may be prompted to enter your passport/Live credentials that you use in your Windows Phone. There might be some information that needs to be completed about you or your phone. Please do so. Then you will be taken to the My Phone landing page.

From this landing page, you will be able to see some of the pictures that you uploaded into SkyDrive (a part of Live services online and the cloud storage for your pictures and

Office documents). You can go into SkyDrive to see your pictures… as described before, your pictures are automatically being backed up to the cloud right after you take these pictures and they are safely kept in there so you don't lose them, ever. Your Xbox LIVE information is also displayed here; you can also go into Office.live.com from here and create documents that will automatically show up on your smartphone. Your Live account's contacts, calendar and inbox can be accessed from here by clicking on the corresponding links.

You will also note that there is a small map of the location in which your phone was last found (you may need to activate this feature manually). This is where your Windows Phone tells you where it is and the last time it reported its location back to you… pretty nifty. You can see in better detail, the map and location of your phone if you click on "Find My Phone". You can refresh this information and your phone (as long as it is turned on and with this service active), will refresh the last location and report it back to you. Now, I know some people may be concerned about "big brother" knowing your location and all, and it is very simple to turn this feature off if you wish to. But think about having lost your phone or if it was stolen, this would tell you where the phone is located.

If you lost your phone at home or your kids may have been playing with it and may have hidden it somewhere at home, you can click on "Ring". This will ring your phone remotely. This is equivalent to calling yourself, but in this case a special ringtone (loud enough) will ring, so you can find it.

Ultimately, if you lost your phone you don't want anyone accessing the information on it. Wouldn't it be great if you were able to lock it remotely, setup a password and ask the good Samaritan that found it; to kindly call you back at the number where you are so you can go pick it up? Well, that would not turn out to be such a bad day after all, because this web service can do that! Click on the "Lock" link on the webpage and you will be able to enter a message for the person that has the phone in their hands. This is a short message (up to 160 characters) so you can tell that person to please call the owner at the number where you are right now (or to leave a message at your home number). You also need to provide with a 4 digit PIN number to act as a password (until you unlock it). You also get the chance to ring the phone while it is being locked out… so that if nobody picked it up, then they will see what to do. Additionally, you need to provide with an email address so that the instructions on how to unlock your phone can be sent to you (just to make sure you know what to do when you get to your phone). When you are done, all you need to do is press the "Lock" button at the end of the form.

If you lost your phone and you gave up on recovering it, then you should probably wipe it clean so that no one can access the information in it. You can do so by clicking on "Erase". A confirmation form will appear on the page so you give confirmation that you want the phone wiped clean of all your information. Check the "Yes, Erase my phone immediately" checkbox and then click on "Erase". Your phone will be completely erased back to factory settings while your information in your live account will still be intact. You will be able to transfer all your account's information from your old phone into your new phone.

In addition to My Phone and Find My Phone you have the "Account" page. From this page you can see all the apps you ever purchased or downloaded with the dates in which that download occurred. Right next to each of the apps that you ever installed onto your Windows Phone there is a link to "Reinstall" where you can click and the app will be sent to your phone for being reinstalled. Additionally to your installed apps, you can also edit your payment information so when you purchase from the Marketplace you are charged to your payment method of choice. One option available for payment (aside from the typical methods of payment) is to pay through your cell phone bill. This means that you will be charged for the apps and music you purchase when you have to pay for your cell phone. One or two years from now, when your cell phone contract expires, if you want to get rid of your current smartphone in exchange for the next Windows Phone available, you can remove a particular phone from an account. This way you can flag the phone so it cannot be used to purchase apps or music in your name.

Chapter 6: Your Windows Phone As Your Social Guru

Before Windows Phone existed, the only truly social activity you could expect to have on your phone was your cellular network. There were plenty of ways to connect to your social networks of choice, but you were just not going to find a single mobile OS with embedded social network features. All mobile OSs started up as a collection of apps that let you perform actions. These apps are presented to you in the form of icons that lead to them. These apps give you a somewhat watered down flavor of your social network. That's it.

Facebook and Twitter have plenty of client apps that connect into their services from all mobile platforms. Facebook in particular is great in releasing apps for almost all mobile OSs. This is quite a feat for Facebook, which ends up partnering up with each OS developer and readies those apps before the actual OS launch. Twitter takes a bit more time to develop their "official app", but they have quite a following among developers that they take care of building the unofficial apps that provide almost all of the networks' services at OS launch time. Other social networks are less active in the development arena trusting their users simply browse into their network from their mobile browsers.

Enter Windows Phone OS in the fall of 2010 (actually, it was earlier with beta and developer phones) and the whole mobile OS is shaken to its core by adding a revolutionary method of integrating social networks into the OS itself. Until that point, no one had turned up with a successful solution for interacting on your social networks from your smartphone. What Microsoft achieved after thorough research is nothing short of spectacular. This is so much the case, that shortly after that, the other competing mobile OSs started offering similar features on their platforms.

In Windows Phone OS you can certainly do what any OS does, you start applications, use them for different tasks, you manage your calendar, you manage your contacts, etc. All those things are handled in similar ways than in any other OS, and then Microsoft took it one step further by integrating information coming from your social networks' feeds.

Microsoft's approach assumes that you are the center of your own set of social networks. Therefore your contacts, activities, actions and interactions are all embedded into the standard tools that come with your smartphone.

Here are some examples:

The most underused feature in mobile OSs is "contact pictures". This feature is great, you get to see your contact's picture on screen if they call you; you can change it as often as you want. However, it implies that you have to go through the work of taking the picture yourself, then adding it to a particular contact. If we are talking about close friends and family members, this may be simple to do, but what if you try to ask an acquaintance about taking a picture to have in your smartphone so you remember what they looked like? That would be certainly creepy (to say the least) and not to mention flat out weird if you ask your boss or a client. A feature that works so well and might be so great should not be undermined by the very same feature that makes it great in the first place! Now, the mobile OS team at Microsoft dared to think one tiny "what if" scenario that changed it all. "What if we connected to social networks that have pictures updated by the users and bring them in as the contact's pictures?" That little thought is exactly what makes good functionality truly amazing. The implication of this "what if" scenario has so much potential that it makes the OS a serious game changer. The result ultimately was that the pictures for your contacts (in your contact list) that are matched to your contacts coming from your social networks are displayed with the picture that the contact itself chose to use to best represent them. If that contact chooses to change their picture in one of their social networks, then the picture changes in your phone when it syncs it up. You may only have a few contacts, but your contacts become "alive" by showing the mood that each person wants to show on their social networks. Microsoft even took this idea another step further by using your contact's "status" and showing you that "contact line". The contact status may come from your Messenger, Facebook and other social networks' status. With this functionality in place, it's not such a big leap to try to use it all over the OS as long as it looks right, feels right and makes sense. What a game changer!

Other examples, in this case of taking the same idea to a whole new level is the "what's new" page in the people hub and the "what's new" page inside the hub for each of your contacts. This page is a collection of the latest posts coming from a multitude of social networks that you have signed in on the phone. If you haven't you simply need to register a new account for the social network under "settings"; "email + accounts" and adding that social network's credentials into the account information. The feeds that this page will use are pictures and status changes posted to your wall or service, ideas, status changes and business-related comments posted to professional networks such as LinkedIn (where you may want to connect to clients and vendors), etc.

Let's see how this simplifies your day: You are leaving to see a client, you get to the client's office, you announce yourself and take out your Windows Phone. You go to your People hub, touch the name of your contact. Slide to what's new and find out that your client has just been promoted to a new position. First thing you tell your contact when you see him is "congratulations on your promotion to...". Think about it, people post plenty of information for you to use and cause a great impression. Some people like me, for example I re-post a link to my articles at Gadgetix.com into my social networks. I've had some people talk to me and said "I read your latest article on x, y, z and ...". Think of it as a great way to break the ice and start a conversation!

On a professional level, Windows Phone OS is already a great tool, but what if you are a grandparent and already retired... Will Windows Phone OS help you too? Well, the same concept of making you the true center of your social networks through your smartphone works for pictures and news of your grandkids (or your family in general). The "what's new" page will still get the latest posts from your children and grandchildren's wall, including pictures and comments. You may see a beautiful picture of your kid on the wall and next thing you know you just tapped your son's name and posted a comment asking him for a copy in high resolution of that picture, which you can take to print at your nearest pharmacy or super-store. If you just want to carry those pictures with you, then you don't even need to ask. You can access and have those pictures automatically download into your smartphone by looking up that contact in the people page in your picture hub. You can access the albums and picture collections and have them locally cached to your Windows Phone device. Again, Microsoft took another good idea and then they took it to a whole new level. Now, let's think about how grouping works with contacts in any contact management tool: You enter your contacts; you group them into somewhat distinct groups… your tool may allow for overlapping of groups (meaning a contact may be a member of several groups if needed). Now, with Windows Phone OS, you can add contacts into groups and define your own. But hey! You might say, what's so different about Windows Phone? Isn't that what you just described that other contact management apps and OSs might do? Well yes! But there is one tiny little detail that you may not be considering… Let's think about how social network integration brings all those contacts into your device, all contacts are the same to your Windows Phone, regardless of the source. Your smartphone doesn't care if you brought contacts a, b and c from your live account and x, y and z from your Facebook. So now; you are able to group contacts from different sources into a group. Not only that, you can access a hub for that group and look into the "what's new" and "pictures" pages in that hub. This integration may seem not worth mentioning, but then again we have the option of looking at one group for your family, your poker night buddies, fantasy football league, and your professional contacts maybe grouped by company name. Any announcements made into any of the social networks made by any of the contacts that are members of that group you created will be pulled into this "virtual wall" that is the "what's new" page in the group hub. You now have the ease and ability of taking a quick look at your client's and his employees announcements all in one shot, plus you can get in a single place the latest pictures of your own family members that may be far away or living five minutes from you…

Another simple way to see your social network notifications is to go to your "me tile" (the tile that shows your own social network feeds). This tile leads into a hub that contains your profile but it also contains a page for your "notifications". This notifications page is another place where you can access any comments made to your profile in the social networks you registered on your phone. The format is very simple: it reports a list of people, as they appear on your contact list with a date of the latest comment they made highlighted in the theme color. Each of these list items is a link into a detail of the particular post made, by whom and the date of that comment. This way you don't need to fire up the Facebook app every time you want to reply to a comment for which you may have received an email from Facebook. As an added feature in the detail page, you can even "like" a particular comment.

A Revolutionary Concept... Now Copied By Others?

It is said that "Imitation is the best form of flattery". If this is true, then Windows Phone OS is definitely setting the trend on binging social networks to mobile OSs. Google's Android OS and Apple's iOS have added or are adding features first found on Windows Phone OS. This is a great validation of Windows Phone OS as the latest entry into the mobile marketplace. Yes, Windows Phone was the last entry into this arena so far, mainly because of the time it took to iron out details and polish the Metro UI, but it is such a revolutionary user interface that it was worth the wait. I don't mean to rant against other OSs, software companies have been copying features since software started being sold... but when the main mobile OSs who own the market start going in the same direction that the new kid on the block is going, that certainly says something!

Creating Social Network Feeds Vs. Consuming Social Network Feeds

So far we have seen examples of how you can consume and benefit from the way Windows Phone allows you to consume feeds that originate in social networks. We have not included the particular social networks' official apps, just the included functionality that comes as part of the OS. Let's focus now on how to create those feeds. There are a few simple ways you can do so and it will take you no time at all.

Status change updates: You can create a new entry-post in your social networks wall or history. This allows whoever is following to you read a quick comment about what is going on in your life, project, assignment, etc. I personally use this type of posts to my Facebook wall whenever I think there is something interesting to say, not everything that happens in my life qualifies for a comment. I do use these to keep tabs of what happened in case I ever need to go back. I also try to keep business and family separate from each other, but sometimes the lines do blend. I have friends I worked with, worked for and who worked for me. I also post some business related comments in my personal feeds and I also do cross posting whenever I post a blog article, I cross post into all my feeds so that it reaches the largest audience possible. This is my Gadgetix.com blog for gadgets and mobile devices, so I use the cross posting technique to promote the website. Unfortunately, this means that if I have you as a contact on my LinkedIn,

Facebook, Twitter and Live.com feeds, you will get to see my post in each and every one of those feeds. Not all I post ends up in all social networks; personal status posts end up going to Facebook, professional posts end up going to LinkedIn or Twitter if they are not related to my blog in which case, it ends up going to all.

The same process applies for posting pictures you have just taken with your Windows Phone. You can have a preferred social network to which you can post with one click after taking the picture, you can have your pictures also automatically uploaded to SkyDrive or Facebook and shared with everyone, your friends or not shared (to be kept as a backup, sort of a Picture Shoebox in The Cloud). In addition to these options there is one more that allows you to "share…" in which case you are presented with all the accounts you registered on your smartphone and you can choose where you want to send it. Your email accounts show up here as additional options in case all you want is to send an email via that particular account to someone in your contact list.

Please note that this social network list is not only going to include the accounts you registered into your smartphone but also the ones you registered into your Live.com account when you were preparing the field prior to your Windows Phone activation.

One great way to post to your social networks in Windows Phone OS is to use Internet Explorer. Once in a particular webpage that you want to share with one of your social networks is to simply go to Internet Explorer's menu and "share page". This action will pop a selection list that will let you choose from several options in which you can share this content with your friends:

- Messaging: lets you send a text message or a Live Messenger IM to one of your contacts. It is equivalent to copying the URL from Internet Explorer, opening Messaging/IM and pasting the URL into the conversation bubble. All you need to do is choose who to send this message to.
- Email Accounts: Each of the email accounts that you setup in your device will appear as a different option as you may want to send this particular URL to your coworkers from your work email account or it may be something you want to send to a friend from your personal email account. In any case, this option completes the URL into the subject and the body of your email and leaves you

the option to either select the email address you want to send the email into or click on the "+" sign and add from your contacts.

- Social Networks: This option lets you post the URL of the page where you are in IE. It shows you a form with a few fields containing the URL (which you can edit if you wanted to); enter a short Message which is limited particularly for supporting Twitter type of short posts and then it lets you choose whether to post to Windows Live (your Live.com account), Facebook, LinkedIn, Twitter or any combination of all of them. This feature is great for posting a single bit of news to all your feeds and while limited in size, it lets you be detailed enough to post a comment quickly.

The same way you can post from IE in your Windows Phone; you can also post from your pictures, MS Office documents, camera (enabling you to post to a social network after taking that prize quality picture).

We have learned so far how to create content from your phone and post it to your social networks. Although posting images (pictures) to Facebook has been copied by Apple, and Google+ integration along with pulling pictures into Android OS by Google's mobile team, these features are not even close to the ways in which you can be in touch with your social networks with Windows Phone OS.

Chapter 7: Your Windows Phone - Preinstalled Apps

I have so far written in detail what some of the apps in your smartphone do. This chapter is where you will find the most detail about all apps bundled with your device's Windows Phone OS. This chapter will not include the particular apps bundled by manufacturers and carriers as they have the right to change them without notice making some details in this book obsolete or even misleading should they change their apps before this book is released.

By now you probably can play around with your Windows Phone. If you didn't so far, please do so. Come back to this chapter after you have familiarized yourself with some of the apps. While you learn these apps, you can use this chapter as your source for "tips and tricks", or you can even go into deep detail while holding your smartphone next to your book (or eBook) and try the features as I describe them.

All mobile OSs (Windows Phone OS is no exception) come bundled with some basic apps. The typical apps included in most mobile OSs are a PIM (a Personal Information Manager) such as Microsoft Outlook on your PC that allows you to manage contacts, appointments and tasks. Other typical tools are email client, music player, web browser, calculator, text messaging and an app store to extend the functionality of your smartphone.

This next section will cover the basic apps that come included in Windows Phone OS. Even if you know the basics of how these apps work, I recommend you to read through. You might read a tip or a trick you never heard of.

Windows Phone Included Apps

Alarms

Your Windows Phone can keep a number of alarms. "Alarms" is the app that allows you to setup alarms. Enter this app and you will be able to setup alarms, you will be able to choose the time of the day, include a message and what days of the week (if it isn't a repeating alarm).

Entering this app will show you the alarm or alarms that are already setup. From this screen you will be able to turn on and off the many alarms you can setup. You turn each alarm on and off by either touching the "light switch" objects next to each of the alarms. Light switch objects work just like a real light switch in a room. The switch is flipped ON when you can see the accent color of your theme inside of the object. When the regular background is visible, it means that the switch is off. At the bottom of the screen there is a "+" round button. Like all menus, you can expand it by touching the "..." left border. This menu in particular has no additional options, so it only expands a few pixels to expose the description of the button in the menu.

Touch the add button in the menu bar at the bottom and you will be able to create a new alarm. The new/edit screen shows you a form you may be familiar with from other platforms (such as Windows, Mac, Linux, etc.) This form requires you to enter the following information: Time, Repeats, Sound and Name. The bottom menu bar shows one or two buttons depending on whether you are creating a new alarm or editing one. You will see a "save" button (with the floppy disk round button) only or save and "delete" (represented with the trash can round button).

Time is used to keep the time of the day in which you want this alarm to ring. Touching the field will take you to a time selection screen where you can slide up and down each of the time components independently: Hours, Minutes and AM/PM. The final result will be in the form of HH:MM AM/PM. When you are done selecting the time for the alarm, you should touch one of the buttons on the bottom menu. The check round button is used for indicating you are "done" and want to use the selected time, the x round button is to cancel the selection and keep the time you had initially.

"Repeats" is used for selecting what days you want this alarm to go off. Touching on this field will take you to a screen with each of the days of the week listed alongside a checkbox. If the checkbox is checked, then the alarm will ring on that day. Special combinations are summarized into the previous screen; for example selecting Monday through Friday will show as "weekdays", and Saturday and Sunday selected will end up being summarized as "weekends", if none were selected, it will assume you want this to be a "one time alarm".

Sound is used for selecting the sound you want the alarm to play when it's time to ring. Touching on the field takes you to a selection screen where all your alarm ringtones are listed. The first option is "vibrate only" in case you want to make this a silent alarm. In all other cases, you have a round "play" button to listen to the ringtone in question. To select the alarm and go back to the previous page, you can touch the alarm name on the screen. The alarm item that is already selected when come into this screen will be displayed in the theme color.

Name is for the name you want to assign to this alarm in order to identify it when you come back for editing. Touch on the field and the keyboard will pop up and let you enter a name to use for this particular alarm. The name of this alarm is going to show in a pop up message/notification message when the alarm goes off.

When you are done with this app you can "back" out of it or just touch the Windows key on your phone.

Calculator

There is not much to say about this app. It is a calculator tool that can work in both basic and scientific modes. When you hold your smartphone in portrait mode and it is a basic calculator, rotate your smartphone to landscape mode and your calculator will not rotate like most apps do, it will transition into a scientific calculator with options to process operations in multiple systems such as binary, hex, oct, etc.

If you use the calculator in scientific mode (landscape) use it in a system other that decimal (for example in binary or hexadecimal) and you rotate your device back to portrait, it will translate the result on screen back into decimal system.

Calendar

The calendar app is a hub that contains different views into your appointments in addition to your to-do list. This app gathers all the calendar and scheduled activities from all your accounts that are setup to sync appointments and to-dos. Your main Windows Phone account; the one you have on Live.com is the main feed for backing up your appointments and to-dos, but you can also enter appointments that will be saved into each of your other accounts. For example if you also have a work account, when you registered it into your device you also went through a step where you had to choose to bring in calendar appointments (which hopefully you checked, if not you can do so now in settings >> email + accounts >> account name, etc.)

The landing hub in your calendar app contains several pages for different views. The page where you land by default is "day". The day page contains a list of the "all day" appointments at the top of the page, then there is a list of the hours in the day, and in the color of your particular calendar (more on this later) you can see what time-slots are taken. A whole day does not fit in one screen, otherwise the font would be too small and unreadable but you can scroll up and down. As you scroll you will see that at the end of one day the beginning of the next is will be listed.

The menu bar consists of 3 round buttons. Today jumps back to today's view in case you scrolled too many days and want a quick way back to the current date. "New" (or the "+" button) will add a new appointment and "Month" will take you to a month view in calendar style. There is one more option if you expand the menu for changing the settings of your calendars.

New/edit appointment is the form you see when you are either editing an existing appointment or you are creating a new one. There are several items in this form. "Subject" is used for the title of the appointment. The location field is used to indicate the place where the appointment will take place. Calendar refers back to the account in which you want to save this appointment, you can choose from all calendars available to you: this means that you can choose one calendar per account you setup plus any calendars you have setup in your main Live.com account. Additionally, you have a date selector as well as a time of day selector both of which look very similar and have a done/cancel round button at the bottom menu. You also have a "how long" field so you can enter how long you expect the appointment to be so it knows whether to block that much time on your calendar. After these fields there is one rectangular button (not part of the menu items at the bottom) that will show more details should you want to see them.

The additional details for the appointment are for setting up a reminder letting you select how much time in advance you want the reminder to pop up in your smartphone or the tool you use on your desktop. How often this appointment occurs (once is the default, every day, every [same week day of the initial appointment], every [same day number of the initial appointment], and every [month and day number of the initial appointment]. Finally, there is one field to choose whether to make this appointment show your time as free, tentative, and busy or out of office.

The settings menu option in your main calendar page takes you to a calendar settings page where you choose the color in which it should display each of the calendars that are available to you. There will be at least one calendar available to you per account you setup to access calendars when you created those accounts for emailing. In the case of your Windows Live account (Live.com or hotmail.com account), you will have access to as many calendars as you have setup to have online. In my case, I have my regular calendar feed, my Birthday Calendar (which is aggregated from the birthdays that Live.com can get from the Facebook and other social network feeds), I also have a US Holidays which is a read-only calendar (Windows Phone realizes that this is read only and does not let you create appointments into this calendar). Each of these calendars can be turned on and off with the light switch control next to each calendar name. You can also choose the color to display each of these calendar items. In my case, I have my work calendar in one color, my personal calendars (including birthdays) in another color and holidays in a different color altogether. Finally, at the end of the page there are two checkboxes for you to choose whether to show to-dos in your calendar (since they have a deadline date associated with them) and an option to show only Facebook events that you have responded to.

The agenda page in the calendar is an itemized list of all the items in your day. Technically there is no difference in one or the other page. Both are lists of your appointments that allow you to choose whichever you like better for displaying your day's activities. If you have few and sporadic appointments you may prefer to see your list in agenda view so that you can see all your daily appointments at one glance. If you have a full agenda every hour or almost every hour you may prefer to see your appointments in an hour-by-hour view as they are displayed in the day page.

The to-do page is a list of items arranged by due-date. Touching each of them takes you to the detailed view for that item. The menu buttons allow you to enter a new to-do or to select several of them (by showing a checkbox next to each to-do). Expanding the menu in this page shows more options available to you such as sorting by priority, showing all that have been marked as completed and settings. Entering a new to-do (or editing an existing to-do) is very easy and you only need to enter a title, due date, priority (selecting from high, normal or low) and optionally enter some freeform notes.

Using the select menu option and checking the checkbox in at least one of the items in the to-do list will show a different menu where you can make all selected as completed (which will take them off your list) or delete them.

The to-do settings page is identical to the settings page for the calendar settings page. You can turn to-do feeds on or off for each of your accounts that you setup in your Windows Phone.

Once in the detail view for a to-do item you can expand the menu to expose some more options than complete or edit. In the expanded menu you will be able to choose to delete, postpone a day or do today a particular task. These are quick ways to edit the dates in your tasks/to-dos.

Camera

The camera app is the one that you would use to take pictures or record video. This app is one of the few that have its own dedicated hardware button. Microsoft minimum hardware requirements for Windows Phones states that all Windows Phones need to have at least one camera and it needs to have at least 5 megapixels in resolution, the hardware specs also indicate that all Windows Phone devices should have a dedicated button with dual action a click at mid-pressure point and a second click when being fully pressed. The requirements and the app make all Windows Phones a viable point-and-shoot replacement camera. Microsoft thought and realized that almost, if not all competing smartphones require users to unlock their screen, select the camera app, then take the picture. When users have many apps installed, this can be a slow process... a smartphone that has a quick "pocket-to-picture" time would have an additional advantage. So, even when your phone is locked out and/or you may be even listening to music or performing other tasks, long pressing the camera button both unlocks and starts the camera app for you. The long press is required to prevent accidentally unlocking your screen. Even though the term used is called a "long press" this means that you only press the button for about one full second before the camera app launches.

Note: If you are security aware, then the last part of the previous paragraph might raise some security questions: unlocking your screen with a button has some security implications. Someone might be able to unlock your screen without knowing your password! Fortunately Microsoft has thought things through and this is not a security flaw that will let someone else access your Windows Phone's information. Pressing the camera button lets you take a picture. That's all. The moment you are done, pressing the Windows hardware key or the Back hardware key, even trying to access the "..." button is not available to you. Any of these actions only get you to the same screen where you need to enter the password to access the rest of your smartphone's features. Your information is safe with Windows Phone.

Here are some tricks you can perform with your camera app:

- Press the camera button half-way to focus and when it makes the "in focus" sound, press the camera button fully for the picture to be taken.
- This is one of my favorites: Touch the screen and the camera will attempt to quick-focus on the place in the image you just touched and take picture. Most smartphone pictures result in a blurry mess; with this feature, it won't be the case anymore! If you are taking a picture by touching on the screen your main subject, just keep your main subject inside the brackets that appear after you touched and the camera will focus by aiming at the subject in question. This is a great option if you prefer to get to the picture even faster and to avoid the subject of your pictures be out of focus. This option works great for fast-moving and sports pictures.

- Touch the "+" and "-" buttons to zoom in and out.
- Touch the back button to see your last picture taken (and keep sliding backwards to see the previous pictures as well).
- Switch from picture camera to video camera by touching the picture/video camera round button.
- Touch the settings to change your camera's settings. I will go into detail about the settings section next.

Taking pictures is as easy as point and shoot (or touch the screen). There are no secrets there. The interesting thing is what you can do with the pictures one you've taken them. If you swipe the screen from left to right after taking a picture, you will go back to review the picture. Additionally you will be able to see a "..." menu to expand. Touch to expand the menu and you will see several options. In this menu you will have options to share the picture (with your social network), use as wallpaper and replace the lock-screen image, delete (if you didn't take a good picture) and add to favorites when you want this picture to be added to your favorites group under the Pictures hub. Use auto-fix to run what other tools call "auto-level" which sometimes makes a picture with high contrasting features more leveled or some colors brighter. If you choose to auto-fix, you can always cancel or undo or save to keep the image auto-fixed.

Depending on whether you are in picture camera mode or video camera mode, you will see a slightly different settings page. The basic settings are almost identical except color effects and resolution. If you ever read, studied or learned any photography you will find these settings very familiar:

- AF Mode: is the mode in which you want to set your autofocus. Even though your camera does not feature a manual focus mode, you can still choose between settings for Macro autofocus and Normal autofocus. If you don't know what these mean, they are used to preset your autofocus in the camera to extreme close-ups (Macro) and everyday pictures (Normal).
- White Balance: is the way to calculate color balancing in correlation to the type of lighting used for the picture. This will help take pictures with more accurate colors. The options are Automatic for automatically balancing whites to the appropriate lighting; Incandescent for times where the lighting being used is

incandescent light bulbs; Fluorescent, for fluorescent light bulbs and tubes; Daylight for pictures taken outdoors on sunny days and Cloudy for pictures taken outdoors on cloudy days. This type of camera being point-and-click, the most logical choice is automatic, but you may want to force some special selections when trying to achieve a particular coloring effect.

- Image Effect: is an option for creating some interesting special effects with your pictures. None will take standard pictures and will not change the actual picture. The other options are Mono, for taking pictures in pure black and white (no sepia tones); Negative for inverting colors in the same way a negative would appear; Sepia is for taking light-brown tinted pictures just like older pictures would be; Antique is for a slightly darker brownish tint than sepia; Green and Blue are for pictures tinted in those respective colors: just imagine the Mono pictures that are in pure black and white but would replace the pure white for the pure color and any other transitioning towards black would be a darker shade of that color.

- Contrast: just like the contrast control on a monitor or a TV, contrast lets you adjust the differential between contrasting colors. The allowed range is Minimum, Low, Medium, High and Maximum, the standard and preferred selection being medium, particularly for those of us who don't want to mess with pictures a whole lot.

- Saturation: The saturation settings refer to how "intense" colors appear to be. The settings options are also Minimum, Low, Medium, High and Maximum. Minimum will produce an almost black and white picture with faint coloring (almost grayish tones) and Maximum for intense and very colorful tones that are set to shine much brighter than their original colors.

- Sharpness: Also ranges from Minimum, Low, Medium, High and Maximum. This option can help optimize borders between shapes ranging from blurry boundaries between contrasting colors to maximum sharpness for sharp borders between colors. Setting sharpness to maximum all the time can render a "Poster" effect, so be careful about setting it this way, particularly in combination with color Saturation. Again, like most point-and-shoot settings medium is where the best pictures can be taken, but for achieving a particular special effect, you may want to play with the extreme settings.

- EV: is for the setting on exposure value. This setting is used for controlling the two primary methods the camera uses to allow how much light comes into the digital sensor: shutter speed (how long the shutter is open) and relative aperture (how wide the shutter is open, which in digital cameras such as this doesn't have much impact). In any case, a negative number will create darker pictures but will increase the shutter speed eliminating the risk of a picture with blurry sections. For example in sport settings, the legs of a runner may appear blurry on an EV setting of 0, but perfectly on focus on -2. Using a large negative value or a large positive value you run the risk of underexposing or overexposing the picture.

- ISO: This setting refers to the film's speed or sensitivity to light. While your digital camera in your Windows Phone does not have any film at all; digital sensors used for digital photography are measured in a similar ISO scale to get equivalent values. A slow value of ISO setting in 50 means that the digital sensor needs to be exposed to the amount of light a longer period of time to produce the same picture than a higher speed sensor setting of 800 (the maximum ISO setting allowed in your Windows Phone). Higher ISO settings are ideal for nighttime pictures but daytime pictures can produce overexposed pictures. Again, you may want to play with these settings but you don't need to if you just set ISO to Automatic.

- Metering: This is a setting that allow you to change the method by which your device's digital camera meters the light in the picture you are about to take. This measuring method is what will determine some of the choices that the device will make when selecting every setting you set to Automatic. There are three methods available, the default is Center Weighted for giving more importance to the amount of light in the center of the picture (this assumes the center of your picture contains the subject of your picture and is not off-center). It does not mean that all your pictures need to be perfectly centered, but it means that the camera will make the auto adjustments based on the readings in the center are of your picture. When using this method the center is usually almost everything except what is on each of the corners. Matrix is the metering method where your picture is divided into a matrix or table where each of the matrix cells have their own metered value and then they are all used to determine the best settings for auto. Spot is very similar to Center Weighted only the area for the measurement is much smaller. This setting will be good for perfectly aligned pictures. Pictures that are off-center will not be measured correctly. The default setting is the one that allows for the widest range of scenarios.

- Photo Quality: refers to the compression that will be given to the picture after it is taken. Higher quality yields larger files that take up more space but look better. A Low quality setting results in smaller picture files that will be of a lower image quality. Higher quality also results in better printed pictures.

- Wide Dynamic Range: Pictures that have highly contrasting colors are difficult to balance when set to all automatic. Most of the cameras will take a picture that allows focusing on the objects in the picture but will lose quality in the details of the most extreme and contrasting colors. Wide Dynamic Range setting ON will take two pictures, one that benefits the detail in the darker object and one that benefits the detail in the lighter object and then combining them. This method allows for a picture that is highly contrasting but still shows all the possible details visible to the rest of the settings.

- Photo Resolution: This setting refers back to the actual Megapixel setting you want to use. My recommendation to you is that you should use the maximum setting possible unless you are thinking of using all of your memory for something else. The higher the megapixel count, the better quality the picture will have when your print it, or the larger it will allow you to print without pixelating.

- Flash round buttons: On the side of your settings menu there are three quick flash settings buttons Flash, No Flash, and Auto Flash. Again, for using your device as your daily point-and-shoot, just leave it in auto-flash.

All the above settings are available except for AF Mode, ISO and Metering when you use your Windows Phone camera for recording video. Additionally, you will find that Quality and Resolution have their own values due to the technical differences between Picture and Video.

- Video quality: Has options for Low, Medium and High. These settings are named the same but they behave somewhat different since the compression used is technically different. In any case, a Low quality video setting will always result in a smaller video file. A High quality video setting results in larger files.

- Video Resolution: This setting also refers back to the actual pixel resolution, however the measurements are done in the same way that TV resolution is made. VGA is used for 640x480 video (similar resolution to standard definition) and 720p HD is used for high definition video. The minimum requirement defined by Microsoft for video capture on Windows Phone is set to 720p, some devices will support 1080p HD as a third option if the hardware supports it.

Uploading videos to YouTube: Windows Phone OS v7.5 allows you to share videos with your contacts via email or into your Facebook or SkyDrive accounts. By allowing you to email videos it also means that you are now cleared to upload your videos to your YouTube account by just emailing them to an email address that YouTube creates only for receiving emails that will be posted by you.

First log into your YouTube account and go to your "Account Settings". Click on the "Mobile Setup" option. You will be presented with an email account that will be setup to receive videos from you. Any emails sent to this email address that happen to have an attached video file will be posted under your account. Copy that email address somewhere and now create a contact in your Windows Phone called YouTube with the email address you just copied. This will help you access this email address by just searching for YouTube instead of trying to remember a long email address.

Now go back to Camera and record any video. When you are done, just swipe back, touch "..." and you will have the option to either "Share", "Share on Facebook" or just "Delete" the video. Sharing will allow you to select the contact (YouTube in this case) and send it to your YouTube account. Remember to send the email as your last step. Sharing to Facebook will automatically share your video to your Facebook wall and make it available to all who have access to your Facebook wall.

Games

This app is one of those apps that blur the boundaries between being a hub for all game apps and being an app itself. The games app is accessible through the Xbox LIVE tile in the home page and the Games app in the app list. Although covered earlier, this app is nothing more than a link to game apps plus a few more pages that show your Xbox LIVE avatar and other information, Gamerscore and promotional information about other games you might be interested in discovering.

There are several pages to this top level Games hub. I will go into detail through each of them and their sub-pages next.

All the Games pivot pages have the same menu items. The menu is only visible when pressing the "..." button at the bottom right corner. The refresh menu option updates all the information from the servers online. The **Settings** option takes you to a page where you can change your privacy settings for the Xbox LIVE service. The Settings Games page shows several controls grouped into several light switch controls. The first one is "Connect with Xbox LIVE". This option when turned on will upload game scores and achievements to the Xbox LIVE servers and displays your gamer profile info. It essentially enables the whole functionality provided in Xbox LIVE services. Next is "Sync game requests". Eventually, you can compete with "friends" that you may find online or your own family and friends may have created online. When turned on, this option lets you automatically try to fetch multiplayer game requests from the Xbox LIVE servers. While all games allow for single player mode on your Windows Phone, some have also included a multiplayer mode where you can either compete against another gamer or collaborate. Multiplayer modes have different settings; some are live (meaning that you are both playing at the same time across the web) and others are turn-by-turn based (meaning that one plays and then the other plays their turn). The last setting available in this page is to "Show game alerts" these alerts can be set for whenever it is your turn on a turn-by-turn game or whenever you scheduled a particular challenge to start. Finally you have a link into the Xbox LIVE privacy settings that takes you to the webpage where you can change other privacy settings.

Collection: is the list from which you link into all the game apps that you download into your Windows Phone. The page is split into two lists; one for Xbox LIVE games and the second list is simply called "Other". The Xbox LIVE list contains all games you downloaded that happen to be compliant with the Xbox LIVE standard. This means that the games report high scores into the LIVE leaderboards and they are structured in a way that you earn points that get accumulated in your Gamerscore profile along with "achievements" a way of getting badges that indicate you passed a certain level of expertise in that game. This is in addition to the actual game scoring system that is considered internal to the game. Sometimes, this internal scoring system may have little or no correlation to the actual Gamerscore or achievement points you may have earned. I will go into the scoring structure in more detail later on. The second list in this page is used also to show what games you have but these games do not report back achievements and scores to the Xbox LIVE services. This means that while the game may have its own high score tables online and you may access them on the web; there is nothing tying back your device, your Xbox LIVE account and your scores. This list of "Other" games is what games look like for other platforms. All games are nothing more than a loose group of gaming apps that you downloaded.

Xbox LIVE: this pivot page is meant to show you information about your profile. The information being displayed does not end there... The page shows your profile handle your "gamertag", if you chose one different than your name. It also shows your "name" (you don't necessarily need to enter your real name) and your Gamerscore. If you have an Xbox LIVE account from your Xbox 360, it may show in different colors. The gold account shows in orange along with your Gamerscore points accumulated up to date. The points are updated at the end of each game to your online account and every time you enter this app, it will update the information from the Xbox LIVE online services (if you allowed for it on your settings). In addition to this information you get several links that will allow you to change your profile information.

> **Profile**: touch on your "gametag", your name or your Gamerscore and you will get to the Profile page (in a sub-hub) where you will see your gamertag, your name, your motto, your location and your bio. All this information can be changed by touching on the pencil round button on the menu. If you do so, you will get into the form that allows you to change this information and will have a save and cancel round buttons in the menu bar at the bottom of the screen. Once back to the profile page, you can also touch the refresh round button to have the information you just saved online come back to the device.

> **Achievements**: Each achievement is like a badge that carries a point value associated with it. Your Gamerscore is the sum of all those points. More achievements add up more points that you can use to size up a potential

challenge from someone else. Experienced gamers have somewhere upwards of tens of thousands of Gamerscore points… I am in the lower half of the 0 to 10,000 Gamerscore points. I normally play games, but not too much. The whole idea of this Gamerscore system is that you can find others that have a similar score than you have so that the game is challenging to all players in the game and one player does not have an unfair advantage over the other.

Friends: If you have friended someone, you will get to see them in your Friends page in this hub. The idea of being able to see them here is that you will be able to see the details of their profile. What they've been playing recently, what they like, etc. This page also lists your friends by indicating which ones are online and which are not.

Messages: If you are a "Gold Pass" holder from your Xbox LIVE services (about US $50 per year, prices may change slightly from the time of writing this book), then you will be able to send and receive messages to other gamers that you have friended. This is nothing more than a nicely presented UI for chatting online, but the user interface is very nice and you can strike a quick chat to arrange the next challenge with your friend.

Trick 1: Touching your avatar when you are in the Xbox LIVE page will animate it. You can make your avatar react to your poking on it. My four year old son gets a kick out of poking at dad on the phone.

Trick 2: when you start listening to music, go to the Home Screen and from there go to the Games hub, access the Xbox LIVE page and wait for your avatar to show up… you will see your avatar dancing!

From the Xbox LIVE page into the "Avatar" link will go into the tool that will let you edit the way your avatar looks. Even though all the following settings are set from your Windows Phone, the process actually happens online, make sure that you have a good connection or that you are connected to Wi-Fi when you start this process. Entering the designer for your avatar is something you can do once and forget or you can keep changing every month, day or week. This tool lets you change your features to make your avatar have a similar set of features than you have in real life; it also lets you change your clothing, accessories, choose props, etc. All items displayed on screen are free and there are plenty of items to choose from. If you are looking for a particular prop or an accessory you may need to purchase it from the marketplace. Navigation between screens is done by selecting to move forward and using the back hardware button to go back where you were before. Once you are done changing your avatar, just save it with the save round button at the bottom menu and you are done.

Sliding sideways on the Xbox LIVE page also shows two tiles. They are a quick way to get to your friends and messages sections.

Requests: this is a page that lists any requests you may have received. Game requests and invites and turn requests are displayed here. Once the request comes in you can have it as a reminder to play at the agreed time.

Spotlight: This is a page used mainly for promotional use. Xbox LIVE services pushes to your Windows Phone deals of the week, featured games and other items you may be interested in looking further. Some interesting videos are available in this section such as "Hot Apps" a weekly set of videos that you can see to get the latest apps in the Marketplace.

Internet Explorer

Windows Phone's Internet Explorer is one of the best browsers available. Microsoft has managed to repackage the engine of their top of the line Internet Explorer 9 for PC into a small, yet full of awesome tool. Internet Explorer on your Windows Phone 7.5 runs the same engine that runs on your PC, this means that it runs faster than the competition and with fewer errors. HTML5 is supported on this version.

Internet Explorer has a simplified interface for you to focus on your browsing and not spend any time trying to figure it out. The main screen is composed of the webpage you are browsing. On the webpage and once it has loaded, you will be able to pan, zoom, scroll, etc. These are all the typical features available to a touch browser interface. You can pan or scroll up, down, left and right by touching the screen and dragging your finger across the screen in the direction you want the screen to pan or scroll. You can double-tap anywhere on the screen and you will get an automatic zoom in to a readable size. Double tap again and you will zoom out. You can also pinch the screen with two fingers and you will zoom in. You can keep zooming in with the pinch gesture past the preset zoom in that double-tap gives you. If you zoom in past that point; you can go back to that point by double-tapping the screen. If you double tap after that, you will zoom out completely to the initial full screen mode. Double tap for zooming is a quick way to zoom in and out but pinching the screen gives you much more control over how much you want to zoom in and out. One thing that people normally do is they zoom in to fit a whole column of text from a website. The added bonus of doing this is that you end up leaving out of the screen all the advertising in the columns next to the one you want to read.

One thing to note as a big difference all touch devices have in contrast to regular desktop browsers is that because you cannot "hover" the arrow pointer over the item you want to expand; some websites may not behave as you expect them to. This is a problem specific to all touch devices, however; it is up to the developers of each website to correct this lack of vision and preparedness for new technologies. In my case, our company spent all of 25 minutes it took to correct this problem on our pull down menus. Our website had pull down menus that would expand on hovering over them; all we needed to do was to add an option to allow also pulling down those menus by clicking on them. Although some mobile browsers will not do anything about this issue, (because frankly it is not their fault that someone did not prepare their website for this scenario); Microsoft has taken it one step further again and added a simple feature. If you are over a part of a webpage and you know that hovering will display or react in a particular way, then try doing a quick tap on the object you were supposed to be hovering. This is only part of the features provided by Internet Explorer and other mobile browsers may not work this way.

In addition to the webpage you are browsing, there is a menu bar at the bottom where you can enter the URL (web address) you are trying to navigate into. The menu bar has a "Refresh" round button to the left of the address textbox. To the right of the address textbox is the usual "..." button to expand the menu bar and see other options.

Here is a complete list of features you can use from the Internet Explorer menu:

- **Refresh button:** touch this button and your device will reload the current webpage. While webpages are loading, you will notice that the Refresh button changes to "Cancel" in case you attempted to load a page by mistake.
- **Address bar:** While the address bar in Windows Phone 7 was on the top of the screen, it made more sense to integrate it to the menu bar and make both items take up less space from the viewable area. Using a single bar at the bottom makes more sense because now it is more consistent with the rest of the UI. Touch this textbox and the keyboard pops automatically. Enter the web address in this textbox and press enter. IE will navigate to the address you just typed. While you are typing the web address you are looking for, a drop down (which in this case "drops up" since the address bar is at the bottom of the screen and the keyboard should not be covered by anything) offering possible web addresses and searches just like the desktop version does. You can type a web address (such as "http://gadgetix.com") or you can type a search (like "weather for 33323"). Searches for terms (as opposed to web addresses) will jump into the search app. Your search for "weather for 33323" should give you a local forecast, current temperature and other web search results. Back to Internet Explorer, while your webpage is loading you will see a fine progress bar at the top of the address bar. It will not interfere with the reading of the actual URL, since it will be displayed in your theme's accent color. While the progress bar is showing, your session is trying to load the webpage into the web browser. You can also interrupt the progress by typing a new web address; this is only possible as long as the webpage is loading. After the page has loaded, you can still type a new target destination and browse into it.
- **Expand menu "...":** will display more menu options. Internet Explorer has many options under the menu, so you may need to scroll the menu up or down to get to those options.
- **Tabs:** The tabs option in Internet Explorer works just like the tabs work in the desktop version of Internet Explorer. Tabs let you have several different webpages open at any given time. Go into the tabs option in the menu and you will find yourself in a screen that has one or more tile-sized tabs. Each of them has a thumbnail view of the webpage it is browsing. A "cancel" round button is superimposed on the top-right corner. Touch that corner and the tab is closed.

Close all tabs and you revert back to an empty-page-Internet Explorer. Back in the Tab screen, you also have a menu with a "+" round button for adding a new tab. Touching this button will go back to the Internet Explorer screen but on the new and empty tab which will be waiting for you to type the web address.

- **Recent:** This menu option is the equivalent to the History button in the desktop version of Internet Explorer. All your history kept so far (length depending on your Internet Explorer settings) will display the title and the web address in a scrollable list. Touch on one of them and you will be taken to that webpage. At the bottom of the list there is a menu with a "trash can" round button. This button will allow you to delete the browsing history from your device.

- **Favorites:** This is the screen where you have your links into the websites you consider your favorites. This screen is a scrollable list with a name for each of your favorites. Touch the favorite name you want to browse into and you will be taken to that web address. If you tap-and-hold; a popup menu will show up and give you two options: edit and delete. Tap anywhere but the menu and you will be taken back to the favorites list. If you touch Edit; you will be taken to a form where you will be able to change the name that shows up on the list (the name of the favorite) and the web address (URL) of that webpage's location.

- **Add to Favorites:** Once your browse into a particular webpage, you can have that web address saved into your Windows Phone into your Favorites list. Touch this option and you will be taken to the same screen used for editing. On this screen you will be able to edit the name that will appear on the list. If a web page title exists, it will be pre-entered for you on this field. The web address of the webpage's location will also be pre-filled for you. If you like the name assigned to it, you should not need to do anything else to get your current webpage into your favorites list.

- **Share Page:** Just like all your other places in your Windows Phone where you can share content; you can share this webpage with your contacts via messaging which will let you send a text message, a messenger message or a Facebook chat message. Selecting this option will switch to your messaging app where you will be able to choose who to contact and whether you want to IM them via SMS, IM or Facebook chat. You can also share this page by sending it to someone else via email. Selecting the particular email account will open up the email app. You will land in a new email page with the body of the email already pre-filled with the web address you were looking at. Finally, you can share your current webpage with your social networks. In this case you will be taken to a screen where the webpage title and the web address will be already entered for you. You will be able to type an optional message that will accompany the link and you will be able to select what social network to post this link into. If you touch on the list of social networks you will be able to select from a checkbox list (meaning you can select by checking one or more than one item from the list).

- **Pin to Start:** Just like adding to favorites will add a link into this webpage, "Pin to Start" creates a tile in the start screen at the bottom of the screen where you can choose to move around to the position you want it to stay. Tiles added to the start screen can be removed by touch-and-holding the tile until the remove round button appears and then tapping on the remove button.
- **Settings:** This option in the menu will let you change the way Internet Explorer behaves. For more information, please go to the corresponding section in the Settings chapter.

Tips & Tricks Using IE9 On Your Windows Phone

Here are some of the most interesting tips & tricks from several different sources on the web, and some I discovered myself, to later find out that they were already well known:

- Once you started adding some of your favorites to IE9, you will notice that whenever you start typing the web address will show the favorites that match that particular address, touch the favorite instead of typing the whole address.
- Swipe your finger over the web address if it spans more than the space allowed for viewing. This will scroll the web address inside the address field so you can read the whole address.
- Whenever you are browsing and if you normally compare webpages on your smartphone vs. your desktop's browser you will notice that some phone numbers and addresses sometimes appear as links. This is a feature that also exists throughout the whole OS. Touching that link/phone number will take you to dial and mapping whenever it recognizes the link in question as a phone or an

address respectively. Internet Explorer and Email content are particularly obvious for this feature.

- Similar to right click on a Windows desktop (or Control click on a Mac), you can "tap and hold" on an object to display Windows Phone's equivalent to a popup menu or what is technically called a context-driven menu. The menu options are actions you can take with the actual object in which you did a tap+hold. Images will show a save picture and share picture which will allow you to either save to your phone for later use or share the picture with your messaging and email contacts. Links will show menu options for opening in a new tab, copying the link and sharing the link. In this case there will be an additional sharing option to your social networks where you can post to Live, Facebook, LinkedIn or Twitter.

- When you open several tabs in your session you will be able to switch back and forth by using the menu, displaying the tabs and then selecting them. This can become a bit repetitive if you need to do a lot of back and forth. Instead try pressing and holding the back hardware button (the hardware button to the left of the Windows Phone button). This functionality is used to switch between apps by scrolling sideways. When you have IE open and with several tabs in use, they will appear side by side as if they were independent apps. Tap on one of them to switch faster.

Search (Bing/search hardware button)

You can execute all kinds of interesting searches with the Bing/Search app. It used to be a few years ago that the search app would just post your keywords to your favorite search engine plus it would search in your device for those keywords. You would get all your results in one comingled list. Windows Phone includes several different tools and combines them in a very smart way in your search app. Since this is a Microsoft OS, and the Bing.com search engine is one of Microsoft divisions, the search features in Windows Phone are powered by Bing.

The search app is accessible by touching the magnifying glass hardware button on the bottom right of your device. Instead of finding a bare bones search bar, you are first greeted by the Bing image of the day matching the Bing.com background image for that day. Images come with a few bits of trivia about that image. Right after that you will notice the search bar at the top, and right below the search bar, on the right side, the general location of your phone. There will be a menu bar that contains several round buttons for Scout, Music, Vision and Voice. Expanding the menu bar with the "..." button will show you options for music history and settings.

Here are all the features you can use with this search app:

- **Background Image:** Touch on the squares within the image and a bit of trivia will be displayed, there are usually two to four of these trivia links and they correlate to the image. The image changes every 24 hours, so the trivia that comes along with them also changes every 24 hours. If you touched one of the trivia squares, you can make it disappear by touching somewhere else on the image.

- **Search bar:** Historically and as I mentioned above, this is the most significant piece of functionality for this app, but the roles may be changing as we will see in a few lines. We will repeat the same search that we executed from Internet Explorer in the previous section. Touch on the search bar, which will make the keyboard pop up. Type "weather for 33323" (without typing the quote characters). Press the "enter" key to submit your search. You will be immediately presented with a "Results" hub. This hub is divided into pivot pages showing results from the Web, Local and Images. Each of them will show a number of results. Each of those results will show the title of the webpage, a blurb and the web address. If you touch that item, you will be redirected to Internet Explorer with the selected webpage. Scroll down and you will continue for a few more results, at the end of the list, you will see an option to get the "next web results", "next local results" or "next image results" depending on what pivot page you are on. If no results can be found from the keywords you will see a message similar to "No results for [search keywords just searched]". Bing is a smarter search engine that tries to provide you with what you are searching in a friendlier way. In this case searching for "weather for 33323"it understands that you are searching for the weather near a particular zip code, therefore it checks with its data providers for the current weather in that zip code plus the weather forecast for the next few days. Bing does the same thing on your desktop. Try searching for a more generic term and you will be able to see the difference. Try "grocery store". You will see that there are results in all pages in the results hub. This particular result set will even show a "grocery store" app available in the Marketplace for you to download along with web search results. In the "Local" pivot page, you will see a map with pinned numbered flags. Each of these ties into the result number in the list. If you touch the map you will go to the Mapping app (powered by Bing maps which I will describe under its own app in this chapter), if you touch the flag in the map, the maps app opens centered on that particular grocery store address. From there you can ask for directions or more map-related information. If you touch the list item corresponding to one of the items in the results local pivot page you will be taken to an item details hub. This hub has pages with generic information such as address and a link into the map app again, directions and a link into the map app showing you driving directions from your current location, you will also see a link to the phone number in which case you will link into the phone app and will dial that phone number. The second pivot page will display reviews, a point rating for the item and a list of how many reviews this location received with a 5, 4, 3, 2 and 1 star rating. The next pivot page lists apps from the Marketplace that may be used with this particular item found. The menu for this item detail hub also includes buttons for pinning this location to your Home Screen, Sharing button for sending it via email or messaging and finally a button for adding it to your Favorites. Additionally, if you expand the menu with the "..." button, you will see an option to suggest changes about this item that you will be able to provide to help make the location database more accurate. This option is very useful to help update information when a store location closes or moves somewhere else. Finally, the Images pivot page offers a collection of images related to the search terms you entered in the search bar. Touch one image and you will be able to see a larger image than the thumbnail you were seeing in the previous page.

- **Scout:** Scout is a wonderful addition to the search app. This is the local expert you want to call whenever you travel to a location and want to know where to grab a bite, what to do, where to shop and give you the short version of the local highlights. If you travel periodically, you will certainly appreciate the features offered by Scout. Scout is presented to you in the form of a hub. The Scout hub is divided in pages for "eat + drink", "see + do", "shop" and "highlights". Each of these pages works in a similar way and it has a map on the top of the screen and it has a list of places significant for that particular category. Each of these pages also offers sorting and filtering options underneath the category title: Eat + drink offers to sort by distance, highest rated, relevance and cuisine. See + do filters by events and attractions, events only and attractions only. Shop offers to sort by distance, highest rated, relevance and category. Think how easy it is now: its late in the evening and you just landed in a city you hardly know and instead of trying to find someone recommend you a nice place near you, you just pull out your Windows Phone, search with Scout and you are done.

- **Music:** Press the music button and point the device's microphone towards the music. The song playing will be identified, and you will be offered to either go to the Marketplace/Collection to purchase it or close the music popup. If you choose to go to the Marketplace, you will be sent to either the Music section of the Marketplace or your music collection (based on whether you own the song or not) where you can see details, reviews and other songs in the album where it was released. If you happen to have that song in your collection, you will not be prompted if you want to purchase; instead, you will have the option of playing it. I was very skeptical of this type of service thinking that ambient noise and other sound distortion factors would render the service very inaccurate. I was pleasantly surprised to test it in a noisy restaurant near the bar area and it picked up the song correctly. Even more, the song turned out to be part of a live collection and it picked the song from the correct release album and all. This is an amazing feature (however, if you know the "Shazam" app this is nothing new). The smartest part of this implementation is how it is integrated into the OS so you are directed to your music collection or the marketplace based on whether you already own this song or not.
- **Vision:** This part of the search app is nothing short of amazing as well. Touch the vision button and you jump into a mode where any form of barcode, Microsoft tag, QR code, book cover, music album cover or other product UPC barcode can be scanned. Even further you can OCR text out of a page with text if you wanted to! The scan will present you with one or more products that match that particular description you scanned. Sometimes several books use stock images

and are designed in a similar way, so they may be interpreted as possible items. In this case several options will be displayed. Touch from the resulting list the one you think best matches and you will be taken to a search for that particular item. The search results hub will be filled with information about the item you are searching for. Local will have any information about the item in question if there are any stores nearby that carry it at the time. "Images" will show you image files found on the web for that particular search term. Again, if you touch one of the items listed in those pages you will be taken to Internet Explorer's render of the webpage that contains that information. Back in the Vision page, you also have the option of looking in your history of past searches where all found items will be listed.

- **Voice:** Voice is another incredible feature that is part of this search app. Touch the Voice button and you will be prompted to say what you are searching for. Try touching it and saying "grocery store"... after a brief "thinking" you will be taken to exactly the same results hub you were taken at the beginning of this section; with results for grocery stores found on the web, local results for grocery stores and images related to grocery stores.

- **Music history:** This feature lists the most recent searches you executed that resulted in music matches. A list of all the found items is presented so you can go back either to your collection or your Marketplace to purchase it.

- **Settings:** The search settings page is somewhat similar to the settings for Internet Explorer as so many features are shared. However; enabling location services here is a critical task as so many of these features are location based. The settings page's first setting is the location services light switch control. Make sure this setting is set to "on" if you want to see all the features enabled. Following are several secondary level location based permissions for executing searches. All the following settings are enabled and disabled by checking and unchecking their respective checkbox control. The very first one is send location information for Microsoft Tags. This option is for when you scanned a Microsoft Tag (similar to a multicolor QR code with more features). Sometimes these tags require of location information as the results may be different based on where you are searching for them. Allow search button from lock screen: this setting is similar to enabling the camera button with the screen locked. This will enable

WINDOWS PHONE FOR EVERYONE

you to perform a quick search, be that for music that is playing or a vision search while the phone is locked and not have to waste any time to unlock first. Next is to get suggestions from Bing as you type the search terms. This is similar to getting suggestions from Bing on your address bar when you are about to browse with Internet Explorer. Allow Microsoft to store and use images from vision searches. This enables Microsoft use your selection after an image is scanned to perfect their process of filtering through the results when you use the service. Finally there is a button that deletes history. Pressing this button will remove all prior search events and results from your phone's memory.

Note: It is worth mentioning here that all these methods to help you find either books or songs; play on people's weaker side since they enable us buying music on impulse rather than as a rational need for media and entertainment. Buyers beware! This is one of the reasons why almost all music stores are so successful. It is not a renewed interest in music... it is simply that music stores make such a broad selection available to us and we can more often than not, buy on a whim. The same exact reasoning can be applied for app purchases on the Marketplace. Software is no longer prohibitively expensive and it is readily available so we can simply purchase it in a few clicks.

Maps

The Maps app is very similar to the Search app. It uses the same components except for the way it normally starts. Search starts off from entering, saying or scanning terms. The result is a set of smart results related to what you are searching, where you can find those items if they can be located near you, etc. Maps starts off of a map view of your approximate location (if you have the location-based services enabled). This means that if you are outdoors, your device will determine its position via GPS. If you happen to be indoors and not nearby a window where the global positioning system satellites are in the line of sight, your location will be either an approximation calculated by triangulating from your 3 nearest cellular service towers/points or the latest saved location.

Your app screen is presented with a map on most of the screen, centered at your current location. The map itself can be moved up, down, left and right by touching and moving your screen. Move while touching the screen towards the point you want to move your map. You can "pinch" to zoom in and out, or you can double-tap to automatically zoom in (to zoom out you need to pinch). As you keep zooming in, you will notice your map keeps refreshing and at some point it will start showing satellite imagery. This is the default view: will look like a map with schematics and coloring for different types of roads/highways, and color coded items for the ground/water features along with parks and other mapped items. Aside from your default view you will be able to set your mapping app to always show satellite imagery (if that's what you prefer).

If you turn on your mapping app while you are driving (please ask someone else to do this if you are the one driving). You will see that your map follows you as it keeps being centered at the latest position where the GPS service located your Windows Phone.

In the menu you will find several interesting options. The menu round buttons will be the (now) familiar "Scout" and "Search" tools; additionally, you will see a set of round buttons for "Directions" and "Me". Your menu options will be able to open up by using the "..." button which will also expose several options. Your mapping action features are:

- **Scout:** This feature works just like scout in the Search tool, but you don't need to enter any keywords for searching. You will see the Scout hub showing the "eat + drink", "see + do", "shop" and "highlights" pivot page lists. Each of them showing the information as it was described in the section for the Search app.
- **Directions:** This menu option takes you to a page that shows several objects while still showing your current position. The features in this list have been revamped for the Windows Phone 7.5 upgrade (if you purchased a Windows Phone 7, please upgrade to benefit from these enhancements and the more than 500 other enhancements that come with this upgrade, it's FREE). You will see appearing from the top two fields: Start and End. Start will be pre-set to "My Location" which will use your current GPS location. End is open for you to enter a destination. The app assumes you are trying to get directions from where you are to somewhere else, but you can touch on Start and change the preset location for any address by typing the new address in. Use regular "USPS mailing address" formatting when you type it. For example: "123 Main Street, Sunrise, FL 33323". If your location is somewhere else than the US; you may use

other formatting for your street numbering or the ordering of City, State/Province and Zip Code. Use the formatting that you are used to when writing a street address and Bing will interpret it to your locale based on your GPS position. Once both fields have the information needed, all you need to do is touch the enter key in your keyboard. At this point you will be presented with a screen cautioning you about using this device while driving. Touch on the button and you will be able to see the driving information from the "Start address" to the "End address". The resulting screen shows you a map overview of your starting point. It reports the distance and the estimated time it will take you to get there. One of the benefits of using these services from online providers (such as Bing) is that they also collect traffic information and it can update the estimate total number of minutes taking into account the traffic along the route. Towards the right of the miles and time estimates you will see two icons. The one highlighted is the car, but you will also see there is a "walking silhouette". If you touch on the latter, the route will be recalculated so that the shortest walking route can be used. You will also notice that not only the route distance but the time it will take you to walk that route will be updated. A voice will also announce as you start and pass by each turning point along the route. This is not the greatest GPS tool to use; it differs from the typical GPS device in the way it displays the information. However, Microsoft seems to have the right functionality for this tool, since it talks you through the turn by turn navigation, but it also has right next to each milestone in your route significant points of interest such as "Exxon on the corner", "Burger King on the corner", which is the type of instructions that a friend of yours would give you. For example: "Drive 1 mile east to Main Street, then turn left at the Exxon gas station." Additionally, at the end of your route, it will let you know that if you reached the next street, then you've gone too far. If you want to review the directions list before you actually start travelling, you can manually scroll up and down by swiping the list. Whichever milestone is showing at the top of the visible portion of the list will be the one that is centered on your map view.

- **Me:** Centers the map to the best available approximation to your location. As long as your Windows Phone is in the line of sight to the GPS satellites, it will be very accurate with your location. If not, it will do its best to locate you within a few yards of your real location by using one of the methods mentioned before.

- **Search:** This is a great feature to have. The search bar will appear at the top of the screen. If you type a search term into the search bar, the nearest items related to those search terms will appear in the form of "pushpins" on the map. The best thing about it is that you can simply touch the microphone icon that appears in the right side of the search bar and "tell your Windows Phone" what you are looking for. It works just the same way that Search works when you do search by voice commands, only the results are listed on your map. Once the items are listed, you can touch any of the "pushpins" and you will be taken to the Search detail hub that will be divided in "about", "reviews" and "apps". These are the same pivot pages that were described in the search results. "About" shows you the details of the item found, with links to the address, directions from your current location to that address and phone number which will trigger the phone app and let you call that number. Reviews lists a point score to the location along with comments left by other consumers with their opinion. If you touch the comment, you will be taken to a page with the list all comments. Touching one comment further on takes you to Internet Explorer at the source website where these comments were originally entered (citysearch.com is one of the main sources for restaurant reviews).The apps pivot page will show you what apps you can use to further explore that particular item found. If you have the app that is being proposed, you will be taken within that app to the details of the item found. If you don't then you will be taken to the Marketplace and will be able to either download it free or purchase.

- **Directions List:** Once you go into Driving/Walking Directions mode, you can switch between full map and directions list view. If you are looking at a full screen map with the directions; then you can expand the menu with "...", then touch on the Directions List menu option. If you are on the Directions List view, you can go back to full screen map by touching the "back" hardware button. If you are reviewing the directions list, you can manually scroll up and down by swiping the list. Whichever milestone is showing at the top of the visible portion of the list will be the one that is centered on your map view so you can see your whereabouts if you are trying to review the route beforehand.

- **Search Results:** When you perform a search on your map, the results are mapped for you with "pushpins" on your map. The pushpins are numbered and only the one that you selected (by touching it) will display the actual item's name. Selecting Search Results will switch the view to a full screen list that lists the item number, name, address, distance and star rating. Touching on one of the items in that list will take you to a Search detail hub containing the same "about", "reviews" and "apps" that the search menu option would take you into. You can see a description of these pivot pages in the search feature of this mapping app.

- **Clear Map:** Just as the label suggests, this will clear all pushpins and location items that were overlaid on the map. After clearing the map some of the menu options will naturally be disabled as there are no more objects to select, items to list, etc.

- **Show Traffic/Hide Traffic:** This option will show the traffic congestion on your map. Depending on the coverage in your area, either the main roads or most roads will be now displayed in a series of colors. Green indicates light traffic moving at or close to the speed limit. As traffic gets heavier, the color overlay turns from Green to Yellow to Red to Black. The information about traffic is what allows the driving direction to calculate time to arrival based on how much traffic you will find in your route. Once Traffic is displayed, the menu option changes to "hide traffic" so you can hide it.

- **Favorite Places:** This option in your menu will list all the places that you selected and marked to be added to the favorites list. This list acts and behaves the same way your favorites work on your desktop. When you find a "place", you can add it to your favorites by selecting the round button with the star and a plus. An address that can be confirmed as valid is deemed a "place". Your favorite places list is a list of locations that shows with the Name you assigned to it when you added it to the list plus the address at the bottom. Once the place shows up in your list, you can select it from the favorites list by tapping on the name. In this case you will be taken to the About pivot page that you have already seen in the map app. Under the address title, you will see the address listed. This address is

WINDOWS PHONE FOR EVERYONE

also a link and it will take you to the map view with the selected address centered on the map and showing the name you assigned in a pushpin. Under the directions title, you will see another link saying "from my location", this will take you to the directions feature of the mapping app with the start field pre-set to your current location and the end field (your destination) set to your favorite item. In the menu, you will find a pin, share and remove round buttons along with a menu option to suggest changes. Pin will create a tile on your home screen that will take you to this place. Sharing will let you send this place via messaging or email. Remove will take this item off your favorites list. Suggest changes will let you report changes in the address for the place you found. This is also useful to report places no longer in that address, changes in zip codes or correcting any other item that may not be accurate. When your favorite places list is too long you can take advantage of the search round button in your list screen's menu. The list filters automatically as you type information about the item you are searching for.

- **Hide Favorites:** This option hides favorites from the map when they are being displayed.
- **Aerial View On/Off:** Turning to aerial view is a great feature. You can use it when you are looking for local features that will let you point yourself in the right direction. You can leave this feature on all the time if you want. When you are in map view, you will be able to turn aerial view on, if you are in map view and zoom in to a detailed enough point, you will switch to aerial view automatically. This is because at an extremely zoomed view of a map, the map stops being convenient and would only show you a line representing that street. Once in the zoomed in view, your map switches automatically to aerial view, but the option to turn aerial view off is disabled until you zoom out and switch back to map view.
- **Settings:** The settings screen lets you change the way the mapping app behaves and will let you enable some extra features. The first option you will see is a light switch control to turn on and off the ability to read directions aloud when you tap on the particular step in the directions list. Next there are two radio buttons to control how the map is displayed while using driving directions. The first option makes the map rotate with your current movement direction so that

the top of the screen indicates where you would go if you walked in your current direction. The second radio button is for having north always appearing towards the top of your screen. While driving, this option is less intuitive because when you are driving south it would look as if you were moving backwards on your screen. Regardless of this situation, others may find this option particularly helpful when you read street names off the map, as they would be upside down when you are driving south. Following these controls there is another light switch control to enable the use of your current location. This means that when you open the mapping app it will try to use the GPS to geo-locate you on the map. Using your location also enables local search results and location based functionality. Finally, there is a button to delete the history. This button works just like the delete history button in your Internet Explorer and lets you clear temporary data on your device.

Marketplace

The Marketplace app is one of the most important apps you will find in your Windows Phone. Your smartphone's functionality can be extended by downloading new apps from many different sources. In addition to apps, you can also download games, music and podcasts. Games are nothing more than apps categorized in a special way, but they are apps nonetheless.

Some apps you will find on the Marketplace were developed by Microsoft, others by the device manufacturers or the carriers and probably one of Microsoft's most prized possessions for this platform: third party developers. The Windows Phone development community is one of the fastest growing mobile development communities ever.

When Microsoft launched this platform, it set out to gather as many app programmers as possible. Their reasoning was that the faster apps appear on a new platform, the easiest it would be to attract new consumers. These days, the marketplace is flowing with apps while still being relatively young.

Your Windows Phone can be extended with your own content, music, videos, movies and podcasts. The Marketplace is the app you will use to get to them. You will be able to download content and apps that will let you use the phone in ways that you never imagined.

The Marketplace tile in the Home Screen tells you how many of your installed apps have pending updates. You can download them to update your apps or just ignore them. Even though there are free, free trial and paid apps. All updates to your apps are free. The updates are meant to enhance, correct and fix your existing apps. When you download, you are guaranteed to always download the most recent app for your OS version.

The Marketplace is a hub app. When you first open it, you will see the landing pivot page with a list of categories. The categories are your carrier's AppCenter, your device's manufacturer's Zone, Apps, Games, Music, Podcasts plus you will see a menu with a "Search" round button.

- **AppCenter and Zone:** Link into lists that let you see the apps released by these providers. It is a way that Microsoft allows the cellular carriers and manufacturers feature their own tools for you. Some carriers or manufacturers will differentiate themselves by offering better or unique offerings. Most of the items in these lists are free. Some of them are very useful such as AT&T's "MyWireless"; an app that allows you to track how many minutes and data you have used so far in your billing cycle. Touching each of these categories takes you to the app detail hub. A hub that is divided into pivot pages for Details: where you see the app's description, the price, rating, size of the installed app, publisher, release version number and buttons for installing or sharing via messaging or email. The second pivot page is Reviews. In this pivot page you will find the total number of ratings, the average rating (expressed in number of stars, where 5 is the best score) along with reviewers rating and comments about the app. The next pivot page is Screenshots, where you will see thumbnail sized screenshots of the application which you can tap and see in full screen (swipe sideways to see the next or previous screenshot). The final pivot page is "Related"; this pivot page shows you any other apps that are considered related to this app. Opening a related app will open another app detail hub with these same pivot pages for each app.
- **Apps:** this is the main hub you will get into when searching for apps. You will find here several pivot pages: the first one will be the one that features one app every day. You can select it and go from here to the app's detail hub where you

can download and install or share it. Next pivot page is where you will see a list of categories such as "entertainment", "music + video", "tools + productivity", "lifestyle", "kids + family", "news + weather", "travel + navigation", "health + fitness", ""photo", "games", "social", "sports", "personal finance", "business", "books + reference", "education" and "government + politics". All apps can be found here. Please note that categories such as "music + video" are not the categories in the marketplace where you can acquire music and videos, but the category where you will find apps that will let you consume or produce music and video. Once in any of these categories, you will see another hub divided in pivot pages for top (for the most downloaded apps), free and new (listing the newest apps added to this category). You can see the details of the app you select from these lists in a detail app hub after that.

- **Games:** This section has almost the same structure as the apps hub, but the categories are more game related. The categories you will find in this section are "action + adventure", "card + board", "classics", "educational", "family", "music", "platformer", "puzzle + trivia", "racing + flying", "role playing", "shooter", "sports + recreation", "strategy + simulation" and "Xbox companion". This last category is worth mentioning, particularly because this is a feature that none of the other mobile OSs have and is a big differentiator with the other platforms. Games in this category interact with the features in your Xbox 360. Game action on your Xbox 360 can be controlled or interacted with from your Windows Phone game companion. The inside hub of this category lists pivot pages for Xbox LIVE, top, free and new. The Xbox LIVE games are showcased in their own page because they take advantage of the special features provided by the platform and the Xbox LIVE framework.

- **Music:** Selecting Music gets you to the Zune Marketplace hub. This is the hub where you can access music for purchasing trying, or simply get information about the music. The Zune Marketplace is structured in a very similar way as the App Marketplace. This is a hub that contains several pivot pages, the most important of which is the Genre page where you can start filtering by any of the following genres: "rock", "hip hop", "r&b / soul", "pop", "electronic / dance", "latin", "reggae / dancehall", "world", "country", "classical", "jazz", "blues / folk", "comedy / spoken word", "christian / gospel", "soundtracks", "kids" and "more". Along with new releases, featured and top albums let you find what you are looking for.

- **Podcasts:** Podcasts are a new medium similar to a blog where you will find mostly editorial and opinion articles that can be listened to. Some news outlets also have their own podcasts so you can also find unbiased news. The podcasts hub is divided into pivot pages for featured, top, new and genres. The genres page has a list with the following genres: "arts", "business", "education", "entertainment", "health", "international", "lifestyle", "mediacasts", "music", "news & politics", "religion & spirituality", "science & technology", "sports" and travel". Podcasts in each of the genres are divided into two main categories audio and video. You can subscribe to a podcast (all of them are free) and they will be delivered to your device whenever there is a new item.

- **Search round button:** In any of the main sections listed in the above bullets, you will find the search button in the menu. This search button will search while being context-sensitive. It will search the whole marketplace if you press the button while in the main marketplace hub or will search only for apps if you are inside the app hub, or even search within a particular app category if you are within a category and press the search button.

Does Size Matter?

App count is not everything. One of the main goals Microsoft set for this platform before releasing Windows Phones to the market was to attract developers. In fact, out of all the mobile platforms available; Windows Phone OS has the fastest growth of all in number of developers and even apps. About a year after the platform was launched, the Marketplace had grown from 0 to more than 40,000 apps. The mix of free apps and paid apps is about 50%-50% growing at a rate of more than 3,000 apps per month. Competing platforms have many times over the number of apps, but they have been in the market for several years. In just a year; the Windows Phone Marketplace has achieved a maturity that makes this a robust and attractive platform not only because of the number of apps, but also for the quality of those apps.

There is a metric available from all major mobile platforms that puts size in perspective and sets the tone for future expectations. 20,000 to 50,000 apps in an app store are solid indicators of growth for the platform as well as the marketplace. They highlight that developers are creating profitable apps and are staying with the platform. How long it takes an app store to reach that milestone is also an indicator of success. For example: Microsoft's Windows Phone Marketplace took less than 10 months to reach 30,000 apps since launch while Apple's iPhone App Store took over 8 months and Android store took 17 months to reach the same amount.

In my opinion, once a platform reaches a critical mass, it is no longer app count what matters, but app quality and how easy it is to find the apps one is looking for. When there are 2,500 apps that do practically the same thing; it almost guarantees that one will not get to the last item in the list. How those apps are listed or how you can get to the one app offering the one feature that matters to you out of those 2,500 that are very similar is a key factor. Microsoft has had the opportunity to refine the search and listing features for the Marketplace. Coupled with the ability to find apps on the Internet, it is a clear advantage.

Finally, growth in the Windows Phone Marketplace has reached a point where it is starting to happen exponentially. While it took just 10 months to reach the first 30,000 apps, it just took 6 months to reach the 60,000 app milestone. Even more impressive; it took only two more months to reach the 90,000 app mark (in April 2012). Accurate and meaningful search results in the search features offered by Windows Phone's Marketplace app, the Windows Phone Marketplace website or the Zune software access to the Marketplace is a key quality indicator that lets you find what you are looking for.

Messaging

The messaging app in Windows Phone lets you communicate in "chat format" with your contacts in several ways. Given that you can have a contact's mobile number, Live account or even Facebook friendship; you can chat with that contact in any of those ways. You can Text/SMS them, chat via Messenger IM or chat via Facebook chat. This app, which started up as a plain text messaging app, is now fully integrated to your social media. There even are some potential candidates for future integration such as Skype. Skype is a VOIP and video calling service that also includes chat and text integration. Skype was acquired by Microsoft in 2011 and is already offered in Google's Android OS and Apple's iOS. It has been confirmed that Microsoft will integrate it to its own mobile OS. The first step in this direction was to release the Skype for Windows Phone client app.

Messaging offers a clean and simple user interface where all conversations are grouped by thread and availability. The messaging app can be accessed in several ways. One such way is from the contact detail on your People Hub and touching the link under the mobile phone, Live account or Facebook account for your contact. This will open the messaging app in a ready to chat thread. The main way for accessing this app is through its tile or app list entry. Because you are not selecting who to chat with (so far) you will land in a Messaging hub that lists two pivot pages: Threads and Online; one to select who to chat by selecting the last conversation you had and the other by selecting the contact itself. This messaging hub has a menu with the following options:

- **New:** Touch this button and you will start a new conversation. The initial screen requires that you enter a contact next to the "to" field; start typing a name and an auto-filtering list will show up right below the field. As you keep typing the list will get shorter and shorter. You can scroll up and down that list or you can keep typing. Select an item from the list to add that contact to the conversation. You can also touch the small round "+" button. This button works just like the same button in an email "to" field. It will take you to a list of all possible recipients of this type of message. This means that if you only keep an email address for a particular contact, you will not be able to contact them via the messaging app. The moment you have their mobile phone, have him/her as a contact on Live messenger or friend the contact on Facebook, you will be able to start a chat session with them.
- **Status:** This option lets you change your status on the services you have on your Windows Phone. You will be able to set your chat status on Live messenger and Facebook to "Available", "Busy", "Away", "Appear Offline" and "Offline". In this case all of them change the way your status appears on their respective services. If you choose to be offline, it will effectively sign you off the service until the next time you attempt to access the service or change your status again.
- **Settings:** Takes you to the settings page for Messaging. You will have a light switch control for turning Facebook chat on while on your Windows Phone.

Turning the switch on will enable you to chat via Facebook chat on your Windows Phone. Turning the light switch off disables your ability to chat on Facebook from your Windows Phone and will not list your Facebook contacts as either online or offline. The second light switch on this settings page is for enabling group texting. When this option is on, you will be able to text more than one contact at a time. Some carriers charge extra or a different service fee for text/SMS messages that are sent to several recipients. This switch can be used to prevent expensive mistakes. Finally there is a button that enables you to change the number used for SMS communications. This is a number that is dependent on your cellular carrier and is used as a gateway for sending and receiving text/SMS messages. Do not change this number unless you are setting up an unlocked Windows Phone or are changing carriers while keeping your Windows Phone. Check with your carrier before setting or changing this number.

The **Threads pivot page** lists all your conversations (threads) with the latest bit of conversation sent or received. The items in this list are ordered by date/time from the most recent on top to the oldest towards the end of the list. Each of the list entries also shows the date/time at which that latest entry happened: For items whose latest entry happened today, you will see the time only. For items that happened during the last 7 days, you will see the day of the week in short form. For items that happened before the last 7 days, you will see them listed with the date in short format (month/day). Touching each of the items in the threads list takes you to that particular conversation thread. In this screen you will see the conversation just like you would see it in any chat/IM application on your desktop. Conversation bubbles are displayed in slightly different colors indicating comments made by you or your contact. In each of the bubbles you will also see a date/time sticker at the bottom right corner. If your last conversation with that contact was in any form of IM, such as Live or Facebook, you will see your contact's online status. The menu bar at the bottom of the screen will have a few minor differences depending on what service you are on. The menu options on this screen are:

- **Send:** When you start typing your answer, this button will change from being grayed out (disabled) and become enabled. Pressing this button will send the message through whichever medium you had selected previously.

- **Attach:** You will be able to send an image, or even take an image on the spot when you touch this button. Pressing this button takes you to a screen where you can select from your albums, pictures, etc. The landing screen is a hub that lets you access your pictures or take one if you press the camera button in the menu bar. Once selected, you return to the chat screen where you can add some additional text before pressing the send button.

- **Speak:** This is one of those features that are not advertised enough, but you will find relying on a lot. Select this button and you will be prompted to "Say your message". This is basically a way to dictate your message to your phone, the phone will convert what it hears into text and you will be able to accept it and send it, or asked if you want to retry. This service is amazingly accurate. I have used it to dictate a text message while in noisy environments and I am still to find a mistaken interpretation of what I said. While you could technically have enough time to dictate a whole conversation when stopped at a traffic light; please obey all laws and use common sense. Some states have laws in place that prohibit you from operating a cellular phone in varying degrees (some prohibit texting, while others prohibit talking, or even holding a mobile device on your hand) while driving.

This particular feature is largely extended if you have paired your Windows Phone to the stereo speaker system in your car via Bluetooth. When I demo Windows Phone to people that want to know how useful it is, this is one of those "you're sold moments":

  o   You are driving, listening to the radio, satellite radio or anything else.
  o   Windows Phone interrupts the music on your car's stereo.
  o   Windows Phone asks you if you want to listen to the text message from XYZ.
  o   If you answer "No", that's the end and you resume listening whatever you were listening to without touching a single button, screen or control either from your phone or your car's controls.
  o   If you answer "Yes", then Windows Phone reads it to you.
  o   You are then prompted if you want to reply to it. You are also prompted if you want to listen again, reply or do nothing.

- Mind you, that this is not a free-form conversation, you are prompted exactly what to say for each of these options. "Repeat" and "do nothing" are quite obvious, you get to listen to the incoming text message again or that is the end of your interaction with the phone, again no controls need to be touched or even looked at. Your hands remain on the wheel and your eyes on the road.
- If you decide to reply, then you are further asked to say your message.
- This is the "aha!" moment for everyone I show how this works.
- You just say exactly what you want to send in your message. Whatever words, in whatever order. You are given a specific amount of time or when you paused for a longer period of time; Windows Phone assumes that you are done dictating the message.
- You are then prompted to confirm and send or try again (in case Windows Phone didn't understand exactly what you dictated out loud).
- If you indicate that the message should be sent; the text message is sent out and again, you go back to listening to your program while you still are keeping your eyes on the road and you haven't touched any controls.

Now, because your Windows Phone knows you are in your car (the car Bluetooth system lets Windows Phone know it is a car) Windows Phone takes the additional steps required to do everything with the voice recognition system called Microsoft Tellme.

Further up in the chapter dedicated to settings, you will find out how to activate this feature to be used at any time. Let's assume you have your hands full; picking up your kids, cooking or doing anything that prevents you from touching the screen of your Windows Phone; you can simply talk to the smartphone and (for example) have it reply a text message for you.

- **Switch:** I have mentioned before that you can text, IM or Facebook chat through this app, but how do you change when you are sending a text message to a contact and want to send a picture to their computer? Simple enough, this button will appear in the menu when you have several ways to communicate

WINDOWS PHONE FOR EVERYONE

with that particular contact. Your available options out of this button will depend on how complete is the information you have for this contact. Your options will be texting a mobile number, Messenger (Live IM), Facebook chat, and "more phone numbers" where all of your contact's phone numbers will be enabled as potential text/SMS message recipient numbers.

- **Invite Someone:** This menu option is available to you when you expand the menu by touching the "..." button. If you are used to Live IM or any other type of chat service, then you know you can IM/chat with several contacts at the same time on the same thread. By selecting this option, you will be inviting a new contact to participate of the current thread. Repeat this same action if you want to invite more of your contacts to participate from this conversation.

- **Delete Thread:** Selecting this option will delete the conversation stored under this thread. You will be prompted to confirm whether you are sure you want to delete the current thread from this device and given the option to select to delete or cancel this action. Please note that some services such as Live can be setup to show the conversation on as many devices as you are logged in. So your past conversations that were part of this thread will not be deleted from those other devices, just your Windows Phone.

The **Online pivot page** shows you the list of contacts that are currently logged in and their status to initiate a conversation. This list combines all the contacts you have in all the services you can use from the messaging app. The people in your People hub appear in the online page because they are your Live messenger contacts or Facebook friends and you can start a chat/IM session with them.

Music + Videos

Most of your media can be found in this hub. The Music + Videos app is a hub that will let you access music, videos, podcasts and radio. Additionally you will be able to acquire more music and media files from the exclusive access you have from this app into the marketplace. This hub is divided into several pivot pages containing lists that help you get to your media in the way it comes more naturally to you. The Zune page lists media categorized by type: music, videos, podcasts and radio. You will also see a menu with several music notes on this page; it will start playing music from your available collection. This is a way to take you straight to your own music and start listening right away. Expanding the menu by touching the "..." button will show a Search marketplace option that takes you to the marketplace and enables the search tool within the marketplace. The options categorized by type on this page take you to:

- **Music:** If you have music and you have synced with your computer or if you have already purchased/downloaded songs and albums from the Zune Music Marketplace, you will find songs listed here. This Music hub is divided in pivot pages that group and list music in different ways. It is meant for helping you find the music you want to listen to.
  - o Artists: lists the artists for the songs you own in alphabetical order. The letter selection tiles are available for you to quickly jump to the initial of the artist you are looking for. Right next to each artist/group you will see a "play" round button. If you want to play all songs by that artist you can do so by touching this button. If you want to drill down further into the albums by this artist, you can touch the artist's name. Also note that the first option before listing all albums in your collection for this artist is called "smart dj": this is a way to select from your collection all artists that "sound like the artist" you selected or have a similar style. Other very interesting pages are listed in this hub; you will find a songs page that will have all the songs you have from this artist. The "Bio" page will have some interesting historical facts from the artist in question. The "Related" page will show you tiles for other artists (in your collection and otherwise) where you can explore their songs, albums and purchase them from the marketplace.
  - o Albums: lists the albums in your collection. Again, these are listed in alphabetical order using the letter tiles. For each album, the cover of each album is listed in the form of a tile with a "play" button for quick access to listening. If you want to drill down to a particular song, you can touch the album's name and you will be taken to the songs page. Along with the "songs" page, you will find a "review" page where the album in question is reviewed with expert comment.
  - o Songs: has your whole song collection alphabetically sorted by song name. You can jump to a particular song directly from here by touching the letter tile and selecting the initial character that the song you are

looking for starts with. A "shuffle all" option is offered in case you have no particular order preference and just want to listen to songs in your collection.

- ○ Playlists: You can create playlists on your Desktop and sync those playlists to your Windows Phone. Selecting a playlist is a great way to listen to music selected either by you or a friend.
- ○ Genres: is a great way to listen to a "type of music" without having to build your own playlist. The information about each song has at least a genre that it links into. By grouping all songs of the same genre together your Windows Phone can play music that matches in style. You can "play" here or touch the genre name and you will be taken to the list of songs that match that particular genre.

- **Videos:** This hub contains all videos that were transferred from your desktop to your Windows Phone on your last sync. The pages in this hub are used for listing "all videos", "TV", "Music", "Movies" and "Personal". Specific information for each listing is provided when you touch the video's name or you can play when you touch the video's tile.

- **Podcasts:** are audio and video equivalent to blog articles. Some TV, Satellite and Cable programs are uniquely offered as podcasts as well. There are two ways you can subscribe to podcasts. One is with the Zune software on your desktop. This option lets you setup all your preferences on your desktop and every time you sync you will receive new podcasts if they became available. You can setup a maximum number of un-listened-to podcasts on your device. These options will let you select whether to keep the oldest un-listened-to podcast or to just ignore the ones you missed and always have the most recent un-listened podcast available. Podcasts containing news-related content or that are more time-critical are usually setup to overwrite the existing podcasts (even if you have not listened to them). Other types of podcast where you are more interested in the content itself than the timing of it are usually setup to stay on your device until you delete them or listen to them. The settings for podcasts subscribed to in this particular way are kept on your desktop's Zune software. This means that you will be able to change these settings from your Zune software but not from your Windows Phone. The second way to subscribe to a podcast is available to you in the Marketplace on your Windows Phone. You can select a particular podcast, subscribe and have it sent to you whenever available. The settings for podcasts subscribed to in this particular way are kept on your Windows Phone. This means that you will be able to change these settings from your Windows Phone but not from your Zune software. In either type of podcast subscription you can choose how many podcasts to keep on your device and what order to show them. This is important not only because you will see them listed in one way or another, but also because it will determine which of the podcasts you are keeping will be overwritten when a new one is released. Additionally there is one more setting for your podcasts subscribed to on your device: The default setting is that new podcasts will be downloaded to your device only when you are charging and you are connected via Wi-Fi. This will help you make sure you don't eat up all your bandwidth during normal usage and that you do not incur in bandwidth overage after several podcast downloads.

- **Radio:** All Windows Phone devices have radio receivers to let you listen to FM radio. While you may not necessarily want to listen to the radio all the time, this is an included piece of hardware that comes with all devices. It is just another way to make your hardware work for you. If you carry with you a Windows Phone wherever you go and you want to carry a radio, why carry an additional device. Just carry a set of speakers or a headset and you will be able to listen to the radio wherever you are. You can select a radio station as your favorite station and have that stored for future use. Radio is a very straightforward screen. You are presented with the tuner frequency and you can slide left and right while touching the screen. This will let you change the station to the next or previous station.

The following Music + Videos page is called "History" and simply lists the latest objects used in the music + videos hub as tiles with the most recent first and the oldest items last. History may not list all the songs that you listen to, because there are plenty of ways to choose what to listen to. For example if you selected to start a "smart DJ" for a particular group or to play an album, it will list those actions instead of the particular songs you listened after those actions.

The next page is the "New" page. Much in the same way as with the History page, the New page shows a list of tiles that link into their corresponding items. This list is based, not on the most recent actions you took, but the most recent download activity. The most recently downloaded items will be displayed at the top of this list, while the oldest will be close to the bottom. Selecting one of these items will go directly to playing that particular item.

Finally, the apps page is a list of the installed apps on your device that are registered with Microsoft as able to work with your media content. Once downloaded, you will find here apps similar to MSN Video which has a collection of streaming videos of the day, including news; Last.fm which is a streaming music app; or even the YouTube app that gives you access to the YouTube content with its own mobile user interface for searching and viewing video content. If you have no apps listed here; then it means you have not installed any apps that interact with your media.

Office

Microsoft Office on your Windows Phone is a hub that lets you access all your Office files from your other environments. The Office hub contains several pages where the organization, look and feel and structure allow you to access most of the information you want at the pace that you want.

Even though Microsoft Office exists in multiple platforms such as Windows PCs, Mac OS, and Web (via Live.com, the cloud service Office 365 or even MS SharePoint), Office is an exclusive mobile implementation on your Windows Phone. Google's Android and Apple's iOS do not have a native implementation of Office for their platform. Instead, they have third party applications such as Documents to Go or QuickOffice Pro. These third party Office document editors do a good job editing MS Office documents, but because they are not the actual product, they end up lagging behind functionality that has to be released first in the original product, so it can be duplicated later on. In some cases, support for a specific change takes some time to be duplicated. Such was the case of the file format that Office documents started using with MS Office 2007 several years ago.

In general terms you can do almost everything you would want to do on a smartphone with Office documents. Obviously the screen factor places a huge constraint to what kind of activity you will be able to complete on your Office documents while on your smartphone. The Office app is prepared to create and edit documents from MS OneNote, MS Word, MS Excel and PowerPoint. Additionally, you can use this hub to access Cloud content such as Office Live. Office Live is a free Office document editing service for users who have no Office apps installed on their desktop, complementing this service with SkyDrive and Live email you would get a close functionality match with Office 365 which is an Office document editing online and storage with other cloud server features such as Exchange, SharePoint, etc. for professional use. This last service is paid.

Office for Windows Phone automatically syncs its content with your Live account. Everything you do in Office is immediately synchronized to the web and from there (depending on your desktop settings) potentially to all your environments where you can review, edit or change those documents. Anywhere you go, you will have your Office documents available to you through the Live, Office 365 or SharePoint interface. If you want to keep a document only in your smartphone, you can also choose to store such document on your device alone, just like you might want to keep some documents stored only on your desktop. We will see next how you can use your Office app along with your Live account in order to have most of your documents available to you most of the time and always updated and synced.

When you open the Office app, you land in a hub where the pivot pages have different lists:

- **Notes**: This is a list of your most recent notes entered into OneNote. This tool is excellent. You can use OneNote for keeping quick notes such as your grocery list, just as well as you can use it to take notes at school, college, do research for a project or even give shape to your thoughts in preparation to write a book. This book you are reading was planned, structured and had its research completed on OneNote. While the document itself for this book is a Microsoft Word document; the online research, notes, ideas and web clippings were all handled from OneNote. OneNote is divided in Notebooks and Notes and just like you would have several notebooks where you write down ideas, you can carry this app inside your Office for Windows Phone. This page contains a menu with round buttons for creating a new note, access your notebook list and search your notebooks and notes for anything in particular from any of the sourced where you can have OneNote documents. Additionally, you can expand the menu by touching the now familiar "…" to create a new note or notebook and pin it as a tile into your Home Screen. You will also see how to pin a particular existing note and notebook into your Home Screen later on.

- **Documents**: This is the pivot page where you can access all your MS Word, MS Excel and MS PowerPoint documents. The list contains tiles that show the most recent documents opened. The menu provided in this page also has round buttons for creating a new document (which gives you even a selection of templates to choose from) and a search button which allows you to quickly search your phone, SkyDrive, SharePoint or all your documents in all locations.

- **Locations**: Is the pivot page that allows you to go directly to the location first and then select what document to open. Once you land on that particular location you can even browse through the folders and files you may have created there so you can open a document to read, edit, correct, etc. The menu bar at the bottom of this pivot page has a button for creating a new document, this particular option lets you connect to your company's SharePoint to be able to see, store or change documents that you may keep there. Here you are prompted to enter the web address where your SharePoint is located in order to securely log into it and access your documents and SharePoint applications.

OneNote

From the Notes pivot page you will be able to open OneNote. You can navigate through your notebooks or go straight into a note. When you navigate OneNote structures you will be drilling down until you reach the note that you are looking for. If you need to go back to the previous screen at any time, all you need to do is press one time the back hardware button. If you are accessing OneNote "sections"; these are the ones represented by tabs on your desktop and web versions of OneNote. Once inside a section you will be able to choose between your OneNote pages (or notes). Touching one of those notes will take you to the note you selected. The note content allows for some basic formatting, inclusion of objects such as images, links, audio and web snippets.

OneNote notes are not documents and do not behave as such. Instead of opening a document for editing; you open a OneNote file which may end up containing several different notes and/or structures. This is why there is a different Office hub-page for the rest of the Office documents as they are handled in a different, more conventional way.

While a note is open for editing, and the focus is set on the title for the note in question; the menu shows several round button options. You can pin your note to your home screen by selecting pin, you can email your note with email; in which case you will be prompted to select an email account to send from (if you have more than one account registered in your device). You can also force the note to be synced if you want to, which is equivalent to saying that your note will be saved to your Live account using the space required from your SkyDrive account. You can also expand the menu by touching the "…" button. Once expanded, the menu shows two additional options for deleting and viewing the sync status of that particular note. The Sync Status page shows a Status Result which will show whether Windows Phone was able to sync or not. In addition to the status the page shows when the note was successfully synced last and when the last attempt to sync was made.

While that same note is open for editing, and the focus is set on the body of the note (as opposed to the title); a different menu shows several round button options. These menu options are for formatting and editing the body of your note. In general terms you can touch the menu option to start a new format change or you can select several characters, words or even paragraphs and touch the menu item to change only those selected. The options are:

- **List**: reformats selected text or starts formatting into a bulleted list. If you have selected a bulleted list item; when you select this option, it will remove the bullet and restructure with the flow of the text.
- **To Do**: Lets you create a To Do list by formatting the text into a similar structure than bulleted lists; only at the beginning of each line, it uses a checkbox. Once you have a list of items in your To Do list, you can check your items as you complete them. The great thing about these To-Do lists is that they can be formatted is that you get to keep the items in the list for the next time. For example if you build a groceries list; you can check the items as you place them

on your cart… then during the week as you use up your groceries, you can uncheck what you need. By the time most items are unchecked again, it is time to go to the grocery store again where you check the items as you place them into your cart. To-Do lists can be more complex and do not need to be repetitive, but in any case; you can use those checkboxes to mark whether you completed a task or keep it unchecked if you think you need more work until it is marked complete.

- **Picture**: lets you go into your picture collection and select a picture to be placed in the note you are editing. If you want to take a picture and then add it instead of selecting it, you can also do that by choosing the camera round button from the bottom menu in the picture selection screen. For placing a picture you need to place the cursor in the location where you want to insert the picture; then select the insert picture option and complete the selection. When you are done, the picture will appear in the place where you had originally placed the cursor.

- **Audio**: This option lets you capture audio from your microphone and leave it as part of your note. For placing audio into your note, you need to place the cursor in the location where you want to insert it; then select the insert audio option. At this point the top of your screen will show that you are recording with a button for you to press whenever you are done recording. As soon as you are done recording, a play round button will appear in the place where you had originally placed the cursor. Touching the play button at any time will start playing the audio recorded.

- The menu bar can also be expanded using the "…" button. As usual, this option displays more menu options that were hidden before.

- **Numbered List**: This option is exactly like the bulleted list, only it keeps track of the numbers and lets you show a numeric list.

- **Increase Indent/Decrease Indent**: These options can be used both on paragraphs and list items and sub-items. This way, you can move a whole block of text to become indented to the right or to decrease its indentation. When used in combination with bulleted, numbered or To Do lists, you can create lists of items and sub-items whenever you need to go into further detail.

- **Format**: This option lets you change the way the text looks on screen. Whenever you select text and then choose this option, the selected text will change the way it looks. You can also select this option right before starting to write text, which will mean that the text that follows after the selection will have the formatting features you selected previously. By selecting the format option; a new screen will appear so you can select from text formatting options; for bold, italic, underline and strikethrough text or highlight which is going to behave in an equivalent way to using a yellow highlighter on text.

Word

Microsoft Word in Windows Phone lets you create DOCX files that can be attached to any form of e-communication and shared with anyone. Microsoft Office is so massively universal that you can send the document to anyone and they will be able to; at the very least; open the document for reading.

From the Documents pivot page, you can choose your most recent Word document from the tiled list; you can create a new one or search and then open the document. Selecting a new document gives you the option to create a blank Word document or use a template. Your default Word document templates will be for creating a activity Agenda, Modern card, a Modern invite, Vibrant card and Vibrant invite. These are just simple templates that have a minor structure to showcase what can be done in these apps. The templates you have in your device will be dependent on what you want to keep. You can choose to add more templates by adding more items to be synced from your phone into the online Office services.

You will notice that switching between your Windows Phone and your desktop for writing Word documents is seamless. You will also notice there are few options for formatting how the content in your document looks. The most important thing you will find here is that whatever you change in your document will appear and look exactly as you meant it to appear. While the desktop version allows you to change the content and the way it is formatted; your mobile version allows you to change the content and change some basic formatting. This helps you focus on content without the distractions of how it looks while at the same time facilitating better and more accurate syncing options.

Once inside Word you will see a simple interface to write your documents. Most of the screen is left to display as much text as it is possible; the main focus is on writing the content you need to write; for example on a document you just received via email before you send it back with your changes or comments. You will also find a menu bar at the bottom of the screen where some round button options are displayed and eve more appear when expanding it. The menu options are:

- **Outline**: Let's you see the document outline view. Assumes that you are looking at the outline so you can quickly jump somewhere and it gives you the option to do so. The menu area is expanded to take approximately the bottom half of your screen. Then all items from the menu are hidden and a scrollable list with each of the important items in your outline indented and selectable. The indentation between outline items is based on whether the items have been marked with styles corresponding to "Heading 1", "Heading 2", etc. If you were not intending to jump into a different section of your document, you can still view the items and when you are done you can exit by pressing the back hardware button to take you to the previous menu view.
- **Comment**: This is a feature you will most likely find yourself using if you normally are sent Word documents that need to be reviewed requiring of your comments but not changing of the content. You can touch the location where you want to place the cursor or select the text to which you want to add comments and then select this option. A field with your comment will be added to your selected text and within the document you will be able to see a conversation bubble highlighting the text on which you are adding those comments after you have finished. If you normally find yourself rushing to your desktop after you received an email with a document attached, now you can confidently leave your desktop behind and still be able to read and add comments to any word document you receive.
- **Find**: This option lets you find the text you enter in the field throughout the document you have opened. Once the first item is found, it shows you a new menu option to jump to the next occurrence.
- **Format**: This option lets you change the formatting of the text you are working with. As mentioned before, this is a very limited formatting subset of features of what can be done with the desktop and online versions to facilitate focusing

mostly on content. In any case, this option will display a screen where you can choose basic formatting: bold, italics, underlined, strikethrough, increase font size and decrease font size. There are three highlighting options (yellow, green and red) and three basic colors (orange, green and red). That allows you to change, highlight, mark or set some basic formatting that may have to be selected on the desktop or online versions to complete these tasks.

- **Edit**: Some documents may be received or stored on your Windows Phone as "read only". This is something that is normally done to keep users from accidentally changing the original or overwriting it with a different copy of it. In these cases, Windows Phone's Word already knows so and disables editing from the moment you open the document. This button is available instead of showing the menu button for formatting. If you were to make any changes, you can "save as…" and then make your changes or even press this button, effectively enabling it for editing.

- The menu bar can also be expanded using the **"…"** button. As usual, this option displays more menu options that were hidden before.

- **Share…**: This option lets you send back your document after editing or changing it. If you haven't saved it, you will be prompted before you can send it. You can share your document to all your email accounts (if you have more than one) plus SkyDrive. If you choose SkyDrive, then this document is immediately sent to SkyDrive and made available online to you, your friends or everyone online depending on your SkyDrive settings.

- **Save**: If you made any changes to a document, you will be prompted whether you want to save or not. If you want to; you can also open the menu and select this option.

- **Save as…**: As mentioned earlier, this option lets you save with a different name.

- **Open Location**: This option is used for opening a Word document from a webpage or a web location. This is particularly convenient when you are given a SkyDrive web address of a document that was shared to you.

Excel

Microsoft Excel is the spreadsheet app in Microsoft Office. The Excel app in Windows Phone; lets you create XLSX files that can be attached to any form of e-communication.

You can share those files and they can be used in any of the versions of Excel available in the market: Windows Office, Mac Office, Office 365, SkyDrive/Office Live. Microsoft Office is so massively universal that you can send the document to anyone and they will be able to; at the very least; open the spreadsheet for reading. This is even true for users who even have other computer OSs such as MacOS, Linux, Chrome and many others because the file format is known and readable in Office suites from other vendors.

In the Documents pivot page from the Office hub, you can choose your most recent Excel spreadsheet from the tiled list that is shared with Word and PowerPoint; you can create a new one or search and then open the spreadsheet. Selecting a new spreadsheet gives you the option to create a blank Excel worksheet. You can also use a template. Your default Excel templates will be for creating an Expense report, a Golf Scorecard, Mileage Tracker and a Timesheet. These are simple templates that have a minor structure to showcase what can be done in these apps. The templates you have in your device will be dependent on what you want to keep. You can choose to add more templates by adding more items to be synced from your phone into the online Office services.

Switching between your Windows Phone and your desktop for working on Excel spreadsheets is seamless. Just like with Word documents, you will notice the app provides little room for complex formatting. The app is all about doing the work you need to do and completing it. Excel does not intend to be a replacement for Excel on your PC or the web; instead it is a complement to your everyday tools; particularly because the size and resolution required for being able to reasonably see a spreadsheet are far higher than what resolution you may get on a smartphone. In the near future this will change. In the meantime, the current offering is simplified when compared to desktop Excel as Windows Phone Word is with respect to desktop Word. The little formatting you can do is still much better and works in the same straightforward way that Word does.

Excel's screen is divided in three main areas. The top bar includes a function button which helps you select from a huge list of functions. Next to the function button you will see the formula bar. This is a textbox that serves a dual purpose. It is a search bar for functions to be used and it also holds the formula for that particular cell you are editing. The function search feature works in exactly the same way the address bar works in Internet Explorer. As you type, the search shows you a drop down list with whatever functions match your search criteria. The drop down list shows the functions that are being found but underneath each function; you will see a short description for that function. This is a great feature to have, as it helps you find the right function when you need it. The drop down list is scrollable and you can swipe up and down in order to get to the right function. Once a function is selected, it is entered for you on the textbox along with the parameter names you should use. Touch each of the parameters and the whole word is selected. Next you can replace that parameter name with the actual value (just like you would do in Excel on your desktop).

The second and largest area on your screen is taken by the spreadsheet contents itself. You will see the familiar row numbers and column characters used to identify each cell in a spreadsheet. The spreadsheet main area can be dragged up, down, left and right by simply swiping your finger across the screen. Touching on a particular cell shows you the content of that particular cell in the formula textbox regardless of the content being a value or a formula just like Excel does on your desktop. You can select a cell range by first touching a cell and then dragging your finger across the screen. You can also touch the column or row header at the spreadsheet border to select the whole column or row at a time. You can also select several columns or rows this way. You can double-tap the border line between cells on the spreadsheet border so it gets automatically resized or you can drag the border to manually resize the column/row. A spreadsheet in Windows Phone can also be zoomed in and out by pinching the screen.

The third option is the menu bar at the bottom of the screen. Depending on what you do on the main screen area, you will see different menu items appear and disappear. The behavior is purely contextual; if you can complete an action; the menu options for that action will appear on the menu bar.

The menu options are:

- **Outline**: While the menu item is the same, the outline functionality is slightly different than with Word documents. This option shows you the entire list of worksheets fund on your spreadsheet. This way when you touch this menu option, you switch to a list of worksheets from which you can select.

- **Comment**: When you select a single cell, one option that is displayed in your menu is to add a comment. A textbox will appear in the bottom half of your screen and you will be able to enter your comments for that particular cell. Cells with comments are displayed with a triangle in the top-right corner of the cell. If you select a cell that already has a comment, then the area that was used for entering a comment is now going to be used for displaying the existing comment. Touch the comment and you will be able to edit the contents.

- **Sort**: When a cell range is selected, the comment menu option is not displayed and instead you will see a sort button. Pressing this button will take you to a screen that gives you the chance to select what fields to sort by and the order (ascending or descending). This sort functionality can be extended by selecting more than one field to sort by. The resulting ordered range will be sorted by the first field, in the order requested. For those items whose first sort field value is the same, they will be sorted by the second sort order (if indicated). When the comment button appears in the menu bar; this option disappears from the menu bar and it appears as an extended menu option after pressing the "..." button.

- **Find**: This option lets you find the content you enter in the field throughout the spreadsheet you have opened. The cell where that content is found will be selected. Once the first item is found, it shows you a new menu option to jump into the next occurrence of that content.

- **Filter**: When a cell range is selected, the search field disappears and instead you see the filter button. Pressing this button lets you filter a column based on your selection on the drop down that is displayed with the unique values for that column. The behavior is the same as setting a cell to become the filtering title for a column in your desktop Excel. The main difference is that once the filtering is done, the filter button disappears until you select a new (or the same) cell range. Pressing the filter button the next time removes all filters and shows all rows that might have been hidden due to the filter itself. When the find button appears in the menu bar; this option disappears from the menu bar and it appears as an extended menu option after pressing the "..." button. The name of these options are "Apply Filter" and "Remove Filter" which will let you create and apply a filter or eliminate it from your spreadsheet.

- **Autosum**: This button can be pressed to calculate quick and simple results you may need on the fly. Pressing this button will show Sum, Average, Maximum Value, Minimum Value and the count of items in your cell-range. Select a range or place the cursor right below a column with values and press this button and these calculations will be offered to you. Select one of them to have that formula entered to the cell below the range in question.

- The menu bar can also be expanded using the "..." button. As usual, this option displays more menu options that were hidden before.

- **Format Cell**: This option lets you change the formatting of the cell you are working with. As mentioned before, this is a very limited formatting subset of features of what can be done with the desktop and online versions. In any case, this option will display a screen where you can choose basic formatting: bold, italics, underlined, date, money and percent. You will be able to also choose the font and fill color for that cell. Color selections are basic (just like in Word) so that you can highlight or mark a cell for further formatting on your desktop or to be able to send the spreadsheet back via email.

- **Undo/Redo**: These options provide you with the feature to go back a step or if you went back, to go forward a step. While editing formulas, you may encounter yourself changing one of those formulas; so being able to undo a mistake comes in very handy.

- **Share...**: This option lets you send back your spreadsheet after editing or changing it. If you haven't saved it, you will be prompted before you can send it. You can share to all your email accounts (if you have more than one) plus SkyDrive. If you choose SkyDrive, then this spreadsheet is immediately sent to SkyDrive and made available online. You can choose to share from SkyDrive to a contact, all your contacts or make the spreadsheet available to the public.

- **Save**: If you made any changes to a spreadsheet, you will be prompted whether you want to save or not. If you want to; you can also open the menu and select this option.

- **Save as...**: As mentioned earlier, this option lets you save with a different name.

- **Open Location**: This option is used for opening spreadsheets from a webpage or a web location. This is particularly convenient when you are given a SkyDrive web address of a spreadsheet that was shared to you.

Even though Word and Excel are very streamlined applications on your Windows Phone, their best editing capabilities are mostly behind the scenes. You notice this when you are editing an extremely complex document or spreadsheet. When you open that same file on your desktop, your changes are just there and nothing seems out of place or formatted in some odd way. The goal of these apps is to just let you make a quick change or read the information you are looking for and continue with whatever it is that you were doing.

PowerPoint

PowerPoint is an app that will let you see, show and edit existing presentation files but will not let you create a new presentation. Although this particular point seems questionable at best, there are reasons why you would not want to create the content of a presentation in PowerPoint. Instead, you can create the content and outline of your presentation in OneNote and then properly transfer and format on your desktop. OneNote is much better suited for creating outlines and capturing your thoughts. The goal of your PowerPoint app in Windows Phone is that you can make last minute changes to a presentation; quickly edit the content of a presentation that was shared with you via email or even add notes into each slide, but not to set a new background or edit its transitions from slide to slide.

You may want to think of your Windows Phone as your safety net for PowerPoint presentations or if you absolutely cannot live without the ability to create presentations on your Windows Phone, please read on for the instructions on how to do this under the "Save as" menu button. This trick will let you create new presentations

Presentations will be available to you from your SkyDrive or any of the other online services; you can even receive them via email on your device and open them up by touching the filename. When you open a presentation you jump straight into landscape mode. You can rotate your device but the app will only rotate from one landscape mode to the other, it will not show any movement when you hold your device in portrait mode. Opening the presentation takes you to the very first slide. From the first slide you can move forward and backwards by swiping the screen from side to side (right to left movement to advance one slide, and left to right movement to go back one slide) or you can swipe the screen vertically (bottom to top to advance one slide, and top to bottom to go back one slide). Double-tapping the screen zooms in just like you would do in Internet Explorer. You can also zoom in and out by pinching the screen. Tapping the screen once displays the menu bar.

The following actions are available through the menu options:

- **Edit**: This option lets you change the content of the first editable object in the current slide. Any object in the slide that you would be able to click and edit on your desktop, becomes editable in PowerPoint on Windows Phone. The editable item will show a rectangle around it. Touch inside the rectangle and you can change the text within that object. At the end of your edit, you can press the "Done" round button to complete your changes. Additionally; when you are in "Edit mode" (after you touched the edit button once); you have additional menu options:
  - **Done**: Exits from edit mode into "View mode", where you are not changing any components on the slide.
  - **Next**: Cycles through all the selectable objects on this slide.
  - **Edit**: This option is the same as touching inside the rectangle surrounding your item to be edited. You are taken to the screen where you can change the text for the selected item.
  - **Move Slide**: Goes into a list where the current slide is pre-selected where you can drag the selected slide into any position you want it to be. This lets you change the sorting of the slides in the presentation. Additionally; you can select any slide (even the ones different from where you were viewing when you entered this list) and drag those up and down to change the order in which they will display. A menu bar and a "Done" button lets you conclude the "Move slide" session bringing you back to Edit mode.

- o **Hide Slide/Unhide Slide**: This option allows you to hide a slide making it impossible to view while in view mode or when you execute the presentation on a desktop.
- **Notes**: This option lets you type in notes for your presentation that will appear either when you "print the presentation with notes" or on screen for the presenter view on your desktop. The notes editor is very similar to the editor used for changing the text in each text item in the slide.
- **Outline**: When selecting the outline view, you are presented with a split screen view where the left side shows as much as possible of the slide and the right view shows you the title for each slide. Selecting one slide from the outline will display that slide on the left side. You can scroll the slide list to select slides beyond the fold in the screen.
- The menu bar can also be expanded using the "..." button. As usual, this option displays more menu options that were hidden before.
- **Custom Show**: This option is only available when the presentation in question has custom show options enabled. When a presentation is created on the desktop, the author can choose to adapt a single presentation to a variety of audiences. Each of those types of audiences can get its own customized render of the presentation.
- **Share**: With this option, you can send the current presentation via one of the displayed email accounts or share the file with SkyDrive.
- **Save as**: This option can be used to save the current presentation with a different file name than the original filename used when it was opened.

Quick Tips: If you must create a presentation, you should create an empty presentation with a few empty slides on your desktop. This process should take you no more than a minute. Let's call this presentation an "Empty Template", even though it is in fact just an empty presentation. Then save the empty template to your SkyDrive folder. Whenever you need to create a new presentation, all you need to do is open the empty template from your SkyDrive location and remember to "Save as" (instead of saving with the current name). This will leave the empty template untouched on your SkyDrive folder and your new presentation saved. Please note that this is only a mere workaround and there are several restrictions;

for example: you cannot add more slides to your presentation. If you want to have slides to spare, then simply create an empty template with many empty slides.

- **Open Location**: As mentioned in the description above, you can open presentations from specific locations. One of them is your SkyDrive that can have a regular folder structure which you can navigate in order to get to the presentation you want to open.

SharePoint

Most consumers have not had any access to Microsoft SharePoint because it is mostly used in corporate environments to facilitate collaboration between coworkers. This service is also highly customizable and allows for programmers to create workflow applications where a request, for example, is automatically transmitted from user A to user B where user B is required to complete some action and then send it on its way to the next recipient. This type of "workflow" service allows the system to control who is the next person in line to receive the request in question so that any particular request is not dropped, sent to the wrong recipient or simply falls through the cracks. In addition to workflow features, SharePoint allows users to access corporate-sanctioned social networking features that are included with the service as well as manage projects, create intranets, extranets, business dashboards, calendaring tools, member lists and even sharing Microsoft Office files. The idea being that these all add up to the collaboration of coworkers, thus optimizing their interaction and producing better business results.

SharePoint is offered both as a system that has to be installed on a server or as a hosted service that you can purchase from a number of vendors and even as a part of Office 365 in its cloud offering. Microsoft has been adding and enhancing this technology for over a decade.

People

The People app is a tool that would be otherwise known as your "contacts" app. In Windows Phone OS, it is known as "People" or the "People hub". The similarities with a "contacts app" from any of the other smartphone platforms end right there, because the best part of this app is how different it can be from other contact apps while at the same time looking familiar to most users.

The People hub is one of the key apps that make your Windows Phone ultimately yours. This is an app that can show information that will be ultimately important to you since it will mostly show updates and pictures from the people you are interested in hearing from.

This hub is the place where you can find all the information pertaining to people with whom you have contacted within any of your accounts, social networks or simply keep information about.

Whatever the source, if you established an account that synchronizes contact information, then that account is capable to provide information that can be used within your People hub and enhance your experience.

The People hub works as a "contact information aggregator": this means that all the information coming from your various accounts can be grouped by and displayed as if it were an aggregated contact. For example: if you have your best friend's home phone number, cell phone number and email address into your smartphone's contacts; and you have your Live contacts with your friend's home address plus their email address; and you are also one of their Facebook friends: the end result is that Windows Phone OS will put all that contact information together and display it under a single contact entry. It does not change the information about your contact on any of the accounts, but only displays it together to help you find that person and contact them whichever way you prefer to contact them.

The People hub is not just your contact app; it can also tell you what is going on in someone else's life or their latest fun pictures (as long as they posted that information to their social networks). In the "What's New" pivot page, you will see all of your contacts change of status from Live, Status changes, wall posts and pictures posted to Facebook and also the pictures and posts from Twitter. All this information aggregated into that pivot page where you can find out what's new about all your friends, contacts and acquaintances. You will also be able to see other people's contact picture (their latest picture downloaded from their social network) without you having to do anything other than have them as your friend. If one of your friends doesn't have a picture in Live, but he has one on Facebook, then the picture displayed will be Facebook's profile picture.

One of the many pivot pages in the People hub is the "Recent" page where you will be able to see a live tile for each of the 8 most recent contacts you did anything with. Your contacts being displayed are determined based on whether you called them, texted them, viewed their profile (and their individual "What's New" pivot page), emailed them or did any activity that involved selecting any portion of their profile on your Windows Phone. Your recent contact's tiles are also animated; when there is absolutely no activity from your contacts, but your contacts have at least a profile picture; the contact's name on your theme's colored tile will show but will be animated with the profile picture.

Now that we covered the basics about the behavior and functionality in the People hub; we are going to go into more detail for each of the particular sections in it. This hub is divided in several pivot pages: "Recent", "All" and "What's New". At first glance it seems to be a small hub, but the hub's customization gets better the more contacts you have.

Recent

The "**Recent**" pivot page is actually one and a half pivot pages wide, you can swipe from the right border to the left border and it will scroll completely to the next pivot page, but swipe it half way and you will be able to see the remaining half of your "Recent" pivot page. If you can see a set of partial contact tiles on the right side of the screen, then you are seeing the first half of the pivot page; if you can see a set of partial contact tiles on the left side of the pivot page, then you are seeing the second half of it. Your 8 most recent contacts are listed here and they are ordered by how recently you had any contact with them. In this pivot page, you can do only a few things. Tap on the contact and you will be taken to a contact profile hub. For a detailed description of the contact profile hub, please see the next section. Touching and holding a contact tile displays a context sensitive menu with the options to "Pin to Start" and "Edit". The "Pin to Start" option lets you pin the tile on your start screen. When you have already pinned a contact to the start screen, this option will be grayed out or disabled. The "Edit" option sends you to the contact profile hub in "edit mode" which is explained within the

Contact Profile hub section. Until then, you should just know that once you are in the contact profile hub, you can choose how to contact that person. The options are displayed to you as a contact list, but any actionable piece of information is a hot-link. This means that you can touch the mobile number and you will be taken to the phone app and that number will be automatically dialed for you; if you touch an email address; then you will be asked to choose the account from which you want to send your email and a new email will be created with the "to" field selected for you, etc.

The "**All**" pivot page is where your contacts are listed in one long list plus some interesting features such as grouping contacts and editing your own profile.

The first item in the "All" pivot page is a picture taken from your Live profile plus the latest status you may have added to your profile. Touch your profile picture or your latest status and you will be taken to the equivalent of the contact profile hub for your own profile. This is called the "Me hub". You will find a detailed description of the features in this hub further down in this chapter.

The following section is a list of **groups** that exists only in your Windows Phone. In Windows Phone OS, you can create any number of groups and add your contacts into them. This will let you see information about those contacts as a group as well as pictures and other activities. Please see the "Using Groups" section in this chapter for more information.

The "All" pivot page contains a scrollable list with your contacts sorted in alphabetical order. The list can be scrolled up and down by swiping the screen bottom to top and top to bottom. This is a typical Windows Phone OS alphabetical list. Each item is a contact and can be selected by touching the contact. To the left of each contact you will see either a grey square that shows you that contact has no profile picture set or a picture that is being brought into your smartphone via your social network profiles. Touching that contact takes you to the contact profile hub that is described later in this chapter. Just like other alphabetical lists in Windows Phone OS, you will notice that contacts are sorted by name/last name, but they are grouped by their initial character. All starting with A, all starting with B, etc. Each of these groups has a small tile right before the group list's first item where the initial character is displayed as a mini-tile. Touch that tile and you will see an alphabet overlay with buttons; this overlay lets you quickly jump into the first item in the list starting with that particular letter. This feature will become increasingly useful to you as you add more contacts to your device or within your accounts that are used in your smartphone. Characters that are grayed out are disabled because you have no contacts starting with that particular character.

What's New

The "**What's New**" pivot page is one of the most interesting features your Windows Phone has. The "What's New" pivot is where you can see the news coming from all your contacts. As described earlier; this is a pivot page that contains pictures, posts and status changes coming in from different sources. Each of the sources being your many social networks you set up when creating the accounts your Windows Phone device can connect into. This pivot page looks and behaves very similar to your Live homepage (also known as your Hotmail Highlights or Live Highlights), your Facebook wall, your Twitter homepage or even your LinkedIn homepage. These web pages are where you see news from your friends, contacts, colleagues, etc. in a way that you can easily learn what is going on with their lives. Each post in itself may contain images from pictures uploaded or just a comment to which you can either read or read and reply with your own. In some cases you can "like" a particular comment without actually responding. Windows Phone OSs aggregation of these posts is very similar, only you will see where the post comes from. Each item displayed contains a quick view of that item. The title of each post is always the name of the source for that post; such as a Facebook friend or the name of the Twitter account you are following. Next you will see the picture(s) in that post and the text of the post itself. To the right of the post's text you will see a conversation bubble. The bubble may contain a number; this number means how many replies to this comment have been received. If no comments were made to that post, then the "+" sign will appear in the bubble. If more than 99 comments have been made, then it will be displayed as "99+". Finally at the bottom of the post, you will see a reference to where and when the post was published; for example "Facebook 3 hours ago". Touching the picture (when available) takes you to a full screen view of that picture. Swipe it up and down and you will be able to also see the original text plus comments from other users as they replied to the initial post. Instead of touching the picture, if you touch the text in the post, you will be taken to a slightly different view where the picture is displayed as a thumbnail and you will still be able to see the comments posted after the initial text was posted. If instead of doing either of those two options, you touch on the comments bubble; you will be taken to a screen where you can either add your own comment after which you will have to press the "post" button or you can simply "like" the post.

Contact Profile Hub

The "Contact Profile hub" deserves a section of its own. This is because it is a huge part of Windows Phone OSs identity. The Contact Profile Hub is where all the information about a particular contact is displayed. You will land in the "**Profile**" pivot page. The Profile page is what resembles the most to other platforms; this page is used for showing all the information you have about that particular contact. You can see the contact's picture (if you keep one or if this is a contact that posted a profile picture in its own social network profile) along with their latest status and the date of that status post. Right below that information you will see all the information made available to you via their social network's profile along with the information you may have entered into the contact's information you keep in your contacts in your Live.com account. Each actionable piece of information is displayed as a link. For example:

- Call Mobile phone number: touching this link starts a call to the number displayed.
- Text+Chat: let's you start a chat session or send the contact a text message.
- Any other phone number immediately dials that number.
- Write on Wall: posts a comment to their Facebook wall.
- Send email: starts an email session to that email address.
- Map Address: Starts the mapping app centered in the address listed in the link.
- View Website: opens Internet Explorer with the web address listed in the link.

Non-actionable information such as Job Title; Company, Birthday, etc. is displayed grayed out for your information but will not work as a link as there is not much you can do with that information.

The menu bar on this screen lists several options: "**pin**" will pin the contact to your start screen, creating a shortcut into this contact. For example, I have my wife as a Pinned contact in my home screen. This allows me to quick dial/text/chat with her during the

WINDOWS PHONE FOR EVERYONE

day if I need to. Additionally, the tile that is created in the home screen flips and shows her latest picture post to Facebook, her latest status change or how many calls I may have missed from her. It is a really nice, compact and quick way to know what happened while my phone was silenced during an important meeting with clients. The "**link**" option allows you to connect several profiles in order to display them as a single merged profile. One of the side-effects of having access to many social networks is that you could potentially get multiple entries in your contact list from a particular contact. For example; I have my wife as an entry in Live.com contacts, she is connected to me via Live Messenger; she is listed as my friend (and wife) in Facebook and she is one of my contacts via LinkedIn. That would make her show up several times in my contacts list. However; with the option to link contacts she appears only once because all those entries are tied together. Windows Phone OS is pretty good at letting you know which profiles are good candidates for linking into a single profile. The linked profiles screen will let you choose linking profiles, remove linked profiles or chose a linked profile that was not detected as belonging to the same person. The "**edit**" option lets you change the information you keep about your contacts. You will not be able to edit the information that your friends on Facebook entered in their profile as that information can only be changed by them. However, if you keep some of your contacts in your Live.com Contacts list, or your contacts under any of the supported account types (Microsoft Exchange, Office 365, Gmail/Google Apps, and others), you will be able to change that information with the edit option. Finally, you can also delete a contact by using the corresponding option.

The following pivot in the Contact Profile hub is called "**What's New**". This pivot is filtered to the posts and elements posted by this particular contact or that were not posted by your contact but include this particular contact in some form or another (such as when your contact is tagged in a Facebook picture). The actions you can execute in this list are the same than the actions that can be executed from the "What's New" in the People hub.

The "**Pictures**" pivot is the next pivot to the right of "What's New"; this is a list of all the picture collections coming from your contact from the many different albums in their social networks. You will see a moving, active tile with the albums they have setup on Facebook. If you touch this double-wide tile, it will go into a second screen with a series tiles. Each of these tiles represents an album. The tile itself is made up of the most recent picture in each album from your contact's profile. Touch one of the album tiles and you will go into the album where you can view all pictures. If you want to see a picture in more detail, you can touch that picture and see it in full screen. Turn your Windows Phone to landscape or portrait mode to be able to see the picture taking up the whole screen. You can also pinch to zoom in and out.

To the right of the "Pictures" pivot page is the "History" pivot page. In this pivot page you can see all your interactions with this particular contact. Interactions are listed from the most recent to the oldest. At the same time these items are grouped into "today", "yesterday", "this week", "last week", "two weeks ago", "three weeks ago", "last month" and "older". The items in this list are represented with an icon for the particular action. The listed interaction types are Message (showing a conversation bubble), indicating that this action took place in the Messaging app; Call (showing a phone icon), that will dial the number for that contact when touched) and Email (showing an envelope) which will show the particular conversation set of emails.

The "Me" Hub

This is a custom version of the contact profile hub. There are similarities with the Contact Profile Hub but since this profile is your own; it is displayed from a different perspective. The goal of this hub is to let you take actions that will have an effect on your profile or status in your social networks. The hub is divided into three pivot pages: "Profile", "Notifications" and "What's New".

The **Profile pivot** page shows your profile's picture; as you set it in your Live.com account. Touching your picture allows you to post a new profile picture to any of your social networks. This pivot also shows a description (using your theme's color) of the newest item in your social networks; for example: "1 new photo" after you posted a new picture to Facebook. Below this description it also displays your latest status from your latest status post to your social networks; or the caption you typed for the picture you just posted. Below this text you will also find a reference to when that last post actually happened. Touching any of these elements goes into that particular post you did and shows you who commented and what their comments were. Because a picture can be displayed here, you will also have the option to save this picture to your own device with "save to phone" or set it as your Windows Phone's "wallpaper" which replaces the image to be displayed when your Windows Phone is locked out and with the screen turned on. One final option allows you to "add or view tags". Selecting this option allows you to see who was tagged in the current picture, but it also lets you tag people you know but were not tagged to it yet. Even though faces are automatically detected by the system, and you can touch them to set the contact's name to the tag; you can also "add a tag" by using the menu option.

Below your profile picture and the latest social media action you took; there is a link to "Post a message", which takes you to a screen where you can type the message you want to post and the social networks you want that message to appear. This message is nothing more than a "Live status" or "current status" in Facebook; it is called different in each of the social networks you are a member of. In any case, instead of posting your current message to all your social networks one at a time, you can do so here once and Windows Phone does the grunt work for all networks where the status can be replicated.

The "Check In" link below the Post a message link enables you to post where you are based on your current location. This feature lets you post into your wall or status the latest location where you are. Selecting this option takes you to a search of the nearest locations by showing a screen to "pick a place". All places that can be found nearby in Bing Maps or Bing search will be listed. This way you select from a list instead of asking you to type the whole name. If the place where you are is not listed in your screen, you have the option to create one by providing the name, address and optionally the phone number.

Finally, in the Profile pivot, you can set your chat status. This only affects how others see you on Live Messenger and Facebook chat. You can choose to be "Offline" which will disconnect you from the IM service, or you can choose to stay online and select one of the following: "Available", "Busy", "Away" or "Appear Offline". These statuses are self-explanatory and they will appear right below your name for anyone that is connected to you via Live Messenger, Windows Messenger, MSN Messenger or Facebook chat.

The "**Notifications**" pivot page is located to the right of the Profile pivot and it is used to list events that happened in your social networks that may be of interest to you. Each entry in this list will let you know what event took place in your social network. The list items will be titled "John Smith commented on your status", "John Smith likes your comment: 'Pictures of my new Windows Phone'" or "John Smith likes your photo" and will act as links into the details regarding that event. Each of those list items will show the source Live.com, Facebook, etc. and the day in which that event took place. The detailed page you land into from touching each list item is the same page you would access if you are going to see the comments about your status change or picture details with comments from the "What's New" pivot.

The "**What's New**" pivot page under the "Me" hub is just like the "What's New" pivot page for your contact's profile hub, only this one is filtered only to your own posts and elements posted by you or that include your profile (such as when you are tagged in a Facebook picture). The actions you can complete in here are exactly the same you would from the contact profile hub.

Using Groups

As mentioned before, there are no limitations to the number of groups you can create within Windows Phone OS. You can add or remove members from each group as you please and the task is very simple. All you need to do is edit the group and add a contact.

Outside of Windows Phone; Groups are handled in a different way. In fact on each of the many systems that Windows Phone OS has to connect into their groups are handled in a completely different way. Microsoft Exchange uses one form of grouping, plus there also is grouping within Microsoft Outlook that remains within the particular desktop where you have it running, other email servers such as Google Apps, Gmail, and many others use their own form of grouping. To make things worse, there are also groups you can have in your social networks such as Live, Facebook and LinkedIn which are handled in a completely different way. The challenge for Windows Phone OS was to integrate all these different types of groups while at the same time keeping them in sync and displaying them in a coherent and consistent way on your device. Because of all these issues and the potential for creating more conflicts than it could resolve; it was decided that Windows Phone would have no groups in its first iteration. In Windows Phone OS v7.5 a grouping solution was implemented with the caveat that this grouping structure would only remain within your own device and would not be propagated or synced to any platform, social network or email service. This group implementation prevents many conflicts, but it requires that you create whatever groups you would want to keep in your Windows Phone.

Once you created a group and added a few members to that group. You can select it from the People hub. It will be listed at the top of the People hub in the "All" pivot page. Once you are in the Group hub, you will see several pivot pages:

- **Group**: This pivot will display one tile per contact added to the group. Each tile representing a contact and will show the profile page, the name and the latest event, picture or status from their social networks rotating from one to the other continuously. At the end of the group, you will see links for each of the possible actions you will be able to take with this group. For example you may be able to see a link into "**text+chat**", "**send email**", etc. where you will be able to contact all this group's members in one touch. At the bottom of this pivot page you will have the menu options for pinning the current group into your start screen, edit the group and delete the group. If you choose to delete the group, you will be able to remove the group association but the contacts themselves will not be affected by this change. If you choose to edit the group, you will land on a screen where you can edit the group's name and add contacts. You can even select one of the contacts to choose what their preferred phone number or email address will be when attempting to contact all the members in the group.
- **What's New**: This pivot page behaves in the same way that all other "What's New" pivot pages do, only it will display the latest news from only the members in the group.
- **Pictures**: Will display a double-wide tile with pictures collected from all of the groups' members. The tile will rotate the many pictures you have from those members. Following this double-wide tile, you will see listed all the members in this group that happen to have albums in their social networks. Touching the entry of any of these group members will take you to the Albums view for that particular contact.

The typical way to go about groups is to create a group to which you would send emails (for example), so you select the group when you send an email instead of each of the individual members of that group. This is the conventional approach to groups for emailing and contacting people. Windows Phone lets you take this one step further as you may be now used to.

Thinking about how different the Windows Phone OS's user interface is; this actually creates a pretty interesting opportunity. You can have in mind what can be done (or at least what we have reviewed so far), and gives you the chance to create groups so you can take advantage of the tools Windows Phone has to offer.

Let's think about the "What's New" pivot page under the People hub. The more contacts you have, the more events that will be posted in the "What's New" pivot page. You may be interested in reading news from one or another friend and your family members, but will you spend all that time and effort into reading everything everyone you ever connected over a social network post? **I don't think so**.

Let's think about how you may be interested in getting news from your closest friends and your family (you could still apply this concept to any group you would like). The best approach is to create a Family and a Friends group. This way when you get to see the group's "What's New" pivot page, you only get to see the posts coming from those listed in the group and not someone else. This is a very convenient feature when you are connected to a very active social network.

Phone

This is the app where you can place calls from your Windows Phone. Starting this app lands you in a screen where you will first see a history list of all your calls ordered from the most recent to the least recent calls. Each item listed displays a phone round button who the call was placed to and information about the call. Touching the phone button will immediately place a call into that particular contact. Touching the rest of the item in the list launches the "Contact Profile" hub which was described earlier in this chapter. If you want to delete a particular entry in the history list, you can touch the entry and hold that entry until a menu pops up with the option to delete it. Deleting one entry at a time does not prompt you for a confirmation if you are sure to delete the entry or not. Please use this option with caution.

At the bottom of the screen you will find a menu bar including the following buttons:

- **Voicemail**: Places a call into the number registered with your carrier where you can pick up your voicemails. Once connected to your carrier's voicemail system, you simply need to follow the instructions. If you have new voicemails, the button will also display how many you have waiting for you.
- **Keypad**: This option will display the typical 3x4 numeric button grid in all cell phones. After entering a number you can either place the call by pressing the "Call" button or you can "Save" the number to your contacts where you will be able to add the number to an existing contact or create a new contact.
- **People**: This option will switch to the People hub and let you choose the contact you want to call. Once in the People hub, you can go into the contact's profile and select the number you want to dial from the Contact Profile hub.
- **Search**: This option will display a text box at the top of the screen and let you type what you are looking for. Any item in the history list that contains the text you are typing will be listed below allowing you to access the item you are looking faster.
- The menu bar can also be expanded using the "…" button. As usual, this option displays more menu options that were hidden before.
- **Delete All**: After having a phone for a while you may want to clear the call history. You can do this by selecting the delete all option. This will eliminate all entries in the history list.
- **Call Settings**: This option will display your Phone Settings page where you can change the way your phone behaves. The first item displayed is your own phone number (this item cannot be changed here). Following will be the voicemail number. This is the number your phone will dial to get your voicemails. If you have an unlocked device, you will have to call your carrier to get the number you need to enter in this field. Your carrier's customer service can provide you with this information. If your device was purchased for use with your carrier, then this information will already be setup into your device. The "Send my caller ID to" option is used for choosing whom to share your own phone number when you are dialing out. Your available options are "everyone", "no one" and "my contacts". The last option will only show your Caller ID to numbers you dial that are within your contacts. The option for activating/deactivating Call forwarding

is displayed as a light switch object. When you turn this option on, you will be asked to enter a phone number. If you do so, you will be setting your phone for forwarding all entering calls to that particular number. The International Assist light switch is used for enabling a safeguard that will prevent you from dialing international long distance calls by mistake or from dialing while abroad. SIM Security is the final light switch control in the settings screen. This setting will allow you to secure your SIM card (if you are using a GSM carrier). You will have to enter a PIN/password to enable/disable this option.

Pictures

The Pictures hub is another of those unique experiences that Windows Phone OS has for you. This hub is divided into several pivot pages where you will be able to choose your picture collection, see the pictures saved as "Favorites", "What's New" and "Apps". Instead of just building an app to manage your pictures, the folks at Redmond decided to get you much more than that. This app lets you see not only the pictures you keep on your device but the ones you keep in your social networks plus all your images stored under your SkyDrive account. Pictures usually take up a considerable amount of space of your device's memory but the always connected features linking this app to your social networks and your SkyDrive cloud storage solution means you are not really taking up any extra space for the pictures you are viewing from other locations. If you want to, you can choose to store some of those pictures on your device which will take up some space.

Your available pivot pages in the Pictures app hub are:

- The landing page on this app has no title, but lets you choose between all the collections available from your phone. You will see four items listed; touch each of them to go into that particular collection.
  - **Camera Roll**: This collection is the list of all the pictures taken on your Windows Phone. The pictures are listed as small tiles in a list that is four pictures wide and five long. The list is scrollable by swiping up and down. If you have auto upload turned on, you will be able to turn it off from the option in the menu. Touching and holding a picture will display a floating menu with the options for Sharing, Deleting or adding the

picture to Favorites. Sharing a picture enables more than the typical email and social network options. If you try to share your picture you will find options for sharing this picture on to services such as Messaging (via multi-media SMS), Facebook, SkyDrive, Twitter and any other app that registers itself as "able to share pictures" when you install it from the Marketplace. In my case, I usually post into my blog; so I have the WordPress app to post directly into my blog from my Windows Phone; so WordPress appears as one of the sharing options. The more apps you have installed on your Windows Phone, the richer your experience will be as the integration with your Windows Phone is a given. Touching a picture opens that picture in full screen mode (either portrait or landscape). In this screen you can pinch to zoom in and out and you can also swipe sideways to see the next/previous picture. While in the screen where you can see a single picture at a time you will have several options in the available menu. You menu options are to "Share" the picture as it was described above; "Share on Facebook" for posting the picture directly to your Facebook account, "Use as Wallpaper" which sets up the current picture as the picture that will be displayed when your screen in locked; "Delete" will eliminate the picture, "Apps" will take you to the list of apps that are used for editing pictures; "Add to Favorites" marks the current picture as one of your favorites making it available as one of the rotating images to be used in your Picture tile and as the rotating background of the Pictures app and "Auto-Fix". This last option for Auto-fix is what is also known as "Fix colors" "Correct color auto levels" or simply "Auto levels". This is usually all that is needed when a picture is over or under-exposed or a part of the picture is too bright or too dark.

o **Albums**: Lets you access all the images grouped by "albums"; where each album is a logical grouping determined at the service provider of those pictures. The top album is the Camera Roll, which is provided internally. You will be able to create a new album when you are using your Zune software on your desktop by creating a new folder where you can store other pictures. Facebook is another provider of album groups.

All your Facebook albums will be added here although they will only work as shortcuts into your albums on Facebook so they only take up little to no space on your device. Facebook will show all your albums, even the album named Profile Pictures and Cover Photos Now that Facebook has enabled the "Timeline view", any pictures you set up as the cover picture (large picture across the page on top of your Facebook timeline) will be available here. Another service providing album views is SkyDrive. It will show as a many folders as you set up on SkyDrive. If you set up SkyDrive as your auto upload target, you will also see a copy of your Camera Roll listed under "SkyDrive Camera Roll from SkyDrive". This view also lets you get into each of the albums and then get to a particular picture or move by swiping sideways to get to the particular picture you intend of seeing in detail. Additionally, the Albums page acts as a pivot in a hub where the other pivots are the following sections of Date, Favorites and People to be described next.

o **Date**: Selecting this option lands you on the Date pivot page. This page lists all your pictures but grouped by date (month and year) in which the picture was taken. There are no menus on this page. When you touch a picture you land on the same screen where you can see the selected picture in full screen with the ability to pinch to zoom and share the picture.

o **People**: Selecting this option lands you on the People pivot page under the picture hub between favorite and albums. In this page you will see tiles for the people from whom you have recently seen some pictures. You can remove them from this list by touching and holding in which case you will see a "Remove from View" menu that will pop up. If you enter that particular contact's picture collection; you will be able to see an "Albums" page for that contact with all the albums to which you have access. From this point on, the features are the same as explained in the "Albums" pivot page.

- **Favorites**: Favorite pictures are pictures stored on your device. In addition to having these pictures categorized to be in your Windows Phone device, all pictures you mark as favorites are available to the picture rotation in the double-wide tile for pictures in the home screen along with the background for the Pictures app. This "Favorites" pivot page shows tiles for the most recent pictures marked as favorite and at the bottom you will see a link for seeing all the pictures in your "Favorites" category. Under this pivot page you can choose a background for this app which will remain selected or you can select the option for shuffling the background which will select a different favorite picture as the background every time you open the Pictures app.

- **What's New**: The "What's New" pivot in the People hub is very similar to this pivot page; however, in this case, because we are in the Pictures hub, the contents of your "What's New" page will be filtered to show only posts that contain pictures. The features and functionality available to you for the posts that are being displayed is still the same as described above: you will be able to post your own comments to the posts in the list.
- **Apps**: This pivot page in the pictures hub is a list with links into the apps that were registered as "able to edit pictures" when they were installed in your Windows Phone from the Marketplace. Each item in the list will start the app you select so you can use it.

Manufacturer Apps

Each OEM (Original Equipment Manufacturer) has the ability to highlight some software that will take advantage of the hardware that distinguishes their device from their competitors.

These apps are normally offered free of charge. Quality of these apps is often above average as the OEMs stand to lose credibility if they are not good enough. Third party developers are making a strong competitive argument and are setting the bar high, even for free apps.

Carrier Apps

Each carrier also has their own section in the Marketplace to highlight some software that will take advantage of the individual features of the devices they sell; differentiating them from their competitors.

This is a very similar case to Manufacturer-developed apps. Some carriers are providing their customers with useful and smart apps such as apps that report the user how many air minutes and how much data is left in their current billing cycle.

Carriers have learned from user behavior that they are better off letting their customers control their usage (when they have a maximum amount of data/minutes to use). Apps such as "myAT&T" connect into the user's account and get the metrics that are available to the users through their website anyway and let them handle how much use of their monthly allotment they want to use. They'd rather you not incur any overages than go to a competing carrier.

Chapter 8: Settings

All the configurable settings can be accessed from within the Settings app. Settings comes preinstalled with the rest of the preinstalled apps. I particularly wanted this app to have its own chapter as it has a clear effect on how the other apps or Windows Phone in general may behave. The Settings app is divided into two main areas. Each of these two areas represents a different group of settings. These two groups are "System" and "Applications". The System pivot page lets you change the way your device behaves in general. These changes will have an effect throughout the device and may be noticeable within most apps. The Application pivot page shows all the settings you can change for the apps that come bundled with your Windows Phone OS. This includes the settings for the apps described throughout the previous chapter in this book.

Microsoft has done a superb job at concentrating all the possible settings within this app so that you can find them in one place while at the same time made it extremely consistent for you to be able to find the settings for each app within each app. This consistency in design is what ultimately makes this OS predictable and helps you find your way around it because "things are where you expect them to be". While this is reflected throughout the whole Windows Phone OS and all preinstalled applications that are bundled as part of Windows Phone OS, you will only find the settings for the preinstalled apps in this Settings app. Any additional third party apps can be configured within its own settings section. Fortunately, this type of example in Windows Phone OS's design sets the bar high enough for app developers to be as consistent as Microsoft has been.

System pivot page

This pivot page contains a list with the most important settings you can change in your Windows Phone's behavior. As you may have noticed by now, there are no apply, accept, OK or save buttons or their existence is highly minimized. Changing a setting in the detail page for that setting means that if you switch into a different app or you exit by touching the "back" button several times, your settings are already set, so you need to be careful not to change any settings you are not comfortable changing. If you are not, but still want to make sure you can go back to the settings you had before, then you can write those settings down so you won't forget where you were and what those original settings were set to. The System pivot page is essentially a list of functional groups of settings grouped by similar type of functionality. This means that when you look at the title for that particular group of settings you will most likely understand what you can change within that settings page. For example; "Location" is the settings group where you can make all kinds of changes to the services that are used throughout Windows Phone regarding your device's use of GPS-related information.

Here is a list of all the items in the list and their detailed explanation:

> **Ringtones+Sounds**: This settings page allows you to enable and disable sounds and ringtones for your smartphone. There are two main light switch objects on top for Ringer and Vibrate. These allow you to make your device make sounds and vibrate when someone calls you. The controls are independent so you can choose what to use: sound & vibrate; sound & no vibrate; no sound + vibrate; no sound & no vibrate. These different settings allow you to configure your device to your most convenient settings.
>
> **Quick Tip**: If you want to quickly mute your phone you can do so by touching the volume buttons on the side of your device, and then touching the bell/ringer button.
>
> Additionally, you can select the default ringtone for your Windows Phone. The sound when a new text, SMS, IM or chat is received; a new voicemail is detected and a new email is received on your device. In each of these cases, you will be offered to choose from a number of options where you can listen or simply select. There are ways you can produce your own ringtones from your music/audio files or you can even install an app that will set any of your audio files as a ringtone.
>
> **Quick Tip**: You can also set specific ringtones for each of your contacts. If you would prefer to do so, you can edit each contact's ringtone in the contact details page.

Finally, there are checkboxes for you to choose whether you want to hear audible feedback from your Windows Phone when you get reminders, keys are pressed on your keyboard, your device is locked/unlocked, and camera takes a picture plus any other functions.

- **Theme**: This settings page sets the overall look of your Windows Phone. With only two controls you can choose from within at least 18 different looks for your Windows Phone. First you choose the background and whether you will prefer to have a dark or light background. If you have an AMOLED or Super AMOLED screen which lights every pixel independently (as opposed to regular LCD that requires a backlight); you can save battery by choosing a dark background. Since most of your background will be turned to black. With the second setting you can select on this page is the accent color. The accent color is the color that some text and icons will be turned to on most pages. Even though your system and app screens will still be black on white or white on black; the highlighted text will be set to the theme accent color. Please note that some apps forego the consistency of the same look and feel for a background image instead. In some cases the image is so well integrated to the app that you barely notice that the app does not strictly follow Metro UI guidelines.

- **Airplane Mode**: At the core of this page lies a light switch control that turns on and off all radio communications. Smartphones have become such a multimedia powerhouse, that you may still want to use your device during a flight for listening to music, watching a movie, playing games, etc. Turning Airplane mode "On" switches all wireless communications off (cellular calls, data, Wi-Fi, Bluetooth, FM radio, etc). Using Airplane mode is more practical than turning each individual wireless type of communications on or off. Turning Airplane mode off, switches back all your settings just as they were before you turned Airplane mode on. If your airline offers Wi-Fi during your current flight, you can go to the Wi-Fi settings page and turn it on individually. Bluetooth and FM radio allow for the same exceptions during Airplane mode.

- **Wi-Fi**: Wi-Fi is the communication technology that was made popular at the end of the 1990's decade. By 2000, people were starting to purchase wireless cards for their PCs but the standard was slow compared with wired connections. The technology evolved and can now perform at near-wired speeds. It has now become a standard with most mobile devices; including laptops, tablets, and smartphones. Wi-Fi communication chipsets are less power hungry than 3G or 4G communications. On the flip-side, the effective range that can be achieved with Wi-Fi is good only throughout your home/office/favorite coffee-shop. Windows Phone allows you to have Wi-Fi on at all times, turn on upon request or keep it turned off.

The Wi-Fi settings page in Windows Phone allows you to turn Wi-Fi communications on and off. It also lets you choose what networks to setup as preferred and have them connect automatically when present and while having Wi-Fi turned on. When Wi-Fi is turned off (or the light switch control is in the "Off" position), you are not using Wi-Fi, in this scenario, all you see is the light switch and the "Advanced" button. Pressing the Advanced button takes you to a page where you will see listed your "Known networks" (networks you have previously setup and successfully connected into). This list allows you to select items to eliminate them if you choose them. When you have the Wi-Fi light switch turned to the "on" position; you will see a checkbox to select whether Windows Phone should let you know whenever new network is detected. Regardless of what app you may be using, this setting will show a notification on the top section of your screen, which you can select and jump into Wi-Fi settings or just dismiss with a swipe gesture on the notification from left to right. Once you turn Wi-Fi on, all the networks available are listed at all times below the checkbox allowing you to see the signal strength and its status (secure, non-secure, connected, etc.) Selecting a network will attempt to connect into it, if any additional settings, username or password, or additional authentication are required; you will be prompted to enter them. Please see your network admin if you are not sure what to do when you are prompted for a password you may not have. Most shops that offer Wi-Fi access, do so free so you do not have to pay, others require that you purchase a product and print your access password to Wi-Fi on the purchase receipt. While Wi-Fi is turned on; going into the advanced page lets you add a new network to your known networks list. The process is almost the same as actually connecting into a network, where you may be prompted for additional information.

- **Bluetooth**: Bluetooth is another communication technology that enables you to communicate but in this case, it is meant to be used for what is called a personal network. The most common Bluetooth connection is the one you can establish between a cell phone and a headset. This enables you to have a wireless headset to talk through the tiny device that connects to your cell phone transmitting voice back and forth. Because connecting Bluetooth devices are assumed to be close by, the amount of power these devices draw is even less than Wi-Fi. Along with the typical wireless headset, you can establish other types of connections such as Stereo Speakers, In-Car Audio (for using your cell phone for calls, texting, listening to music, etc), and many other functions. All Bluetooth connections require that you "pair devices" or confirm you want to connect those two devices. This means that you will need to enable your Windows Phone into its "pairing mode". In some cases, you will be provided with a code that you will have to type on the second device, and in other cases the pairing will be established almost automatically. This process varies in complexity based on the particular devices to connect. Once a pairing has been established, you can simply turn on Bluetooth on your Windows Phone (or keep it always on) and the devices will pair automatically without needing to pair them again. In the past (and particularly with older devices) the pairing process was somewhat "flaky", and you would have to either restart your cell phone or restart your Bluetooth device (or both). These annoying problems have mostly disappeared but you may see them happening from time to time if you use a Bluetooth device that uses older Bluetooth standards.

Even though you want to save battery, Bluetooth's power draw is so minimal that you can leave it turned on throughout the day. In my case, I leave it on and whenever I get into my car (for example) the car stereo automatically pairs with my phone without having to take it out of my pocket.

The look of the Bluetooth settings page is very similar to the Wi-Fi settings page with some minor exceptions. You will have first a light switch for turning on/off the communication service. If you turn it off, that is all you will see. If you turn it on; your device automatically starts polling for other Bluetooth devices within range. If you have already paired any devices, they will be listed, with their connection status (either connected or not connected). In case your device has not connected automatically, or the other Bluetooth device is not set to automatically connect; touching one of the disconnected devices starts the connection process. Any other devices within range that have not been paired will show a status of "tap to pair". Touching the device name, starts the pairing process. If a PIN is required: for example to pair your Windows Phone with your desktop or your car stereo; you will be prompted with the PIN to type on whichever device is needed. Some devices such as a headset require of pressing the headset power button for more than 3 to 5 seconds to start the pairing mode, and after that offer a series of sounds to let you know that the pairing process succeeded or failed. Please see the other devices' instructions to follow the steps that may be required.

- **Email+Accounts**: This is the settings page where you can add, remove or change accounts into email, calendar, contacts or your social networks. The first screen you are presented with contains only a few options. You will see a button to add a new account, and you will have all your already setup accounts. Touching the add a new account will guide you through creating a new account for Windows Phone, and touching an existing will let you edit the settings for that account. When changing an account, some settings will be read-only. If you followed all the steps when setting up your Windows Phone, you most likely already have a Windows Live account setup in this page. I will guide you through the steps required for setting a generic email account. These steps are for the most part the same only changing where you would provide the specific information about that account.

    Touch "Add an Account". You will be taken to a list where you will be able to select what type of account you want to setup. Some types of account are allowed only one instance. Some services such as social media sites work under the assumption that you will only have one account on their site. Windows Phone follows that same assumption that you own only one social media account of each type (such as LinkedIn, Facebook, Twitter, etc). Therefore, Windows Phone will allow as many email accounts of any type, but only one of each of the social media services.

The types offered by this selection page are Windows Live, Outlook, Yahoo! Mail, Google, Facebook, LinkedIn, Twitter, Other Account, Carrier-driven services (i.e. AT&T Address Book). **Windows Live** is used for setting up Hotmail, Windows Live email, Xbox LIVE, Messenger and other passport-driven services. Your Windows Phone requires of one main account so you can benefit from the integration services, gaming through Xbox LIVE, Marketplace, etc. that your smartphone has to offer. You can add other Live accounts but they will be secondary on your phone. **Outlook** is used for setting up MS Exchange accounts, Office 365 and other email servers that have the EAS protocol enabled. You could setup any Google Apps/Gmail account through this type of account since Google also uses EAS, just remember to enable SSL and use "m.google.com" as the server you will be connecting into. **Yahoo! Mail** is used for connecting into Yahoo! Email services. **Google** can be used for connecting into Google Apps and Gmail accounts although you may want to use Outlook for these types of account since they will be pretty much the same. **Facebook** is used for enabling your social network integration and will bring in all the latest posts, pictures, contact pictures and additional settings as described in earlier chapters. **LinkedIn** allows for integration of profile pictures and status posts/post updates, etc. Twitter will also integrate your Windows Phone with the social network. **Other Account** is usually left for older-type of email servers providing POP and IMAP integration. If you have the possibility of avoiding this type of setup in favor of any of the other types of accounts, please try to. These are older protocols and usually do not offer "full synchronizing" features where you can keep emails, calendars, tasks and other bits of information in your smartphone as well as in your desktop. Finally, **Carrier services** such as "at&t Address Book" are offered by your carrier. Please beware of these services; in this case, this is a service where you keep your contacts stored at AT&T servers. This is a redundant service: you do not need to keep your contacts tied into your carrier any more. While you might have needed for backup with your old flip-feature-phone, this very same service is offered to you free of charge through your Live account which you will setup regardless so you can benefit from the other features your Windows Phone has to offer. You don't even need to keep your contacts stored with your Windows Live account. If you want to keep your contacts in your Gmail account or any other, you could still do so. Your contacts will come from all and any of your accounts that you setup; where you save them, is up to you. Beware of services that you may be charged for. If your carrier wants to charge you for using this service, all you need to do is not set it up.

After selecting the account type; the first thing you will be prompted with will be your user name and password (email address and password). This information lets Windows Phone determine some settings on its own by attempting to connect with this information alone. For example, the server name can be derived from your email address, where your user name can be assumed to be either your email address or the part of your email address that is before the "@" sign. If Windows Phone can establish a connection, then most of the information will be pre-filled for you, if not you may have to provide that information. As a general rule; if you were able to setup your email account on your desktop (of any kind), then you should be able to setup your email account on your Windows Phone. If you still need some help, you may browse on your desktop to http://www.windowsphone.com and click on the "How-to" link at the top of the page. Press the "Sign In" button. If you are prompted with a page to check your credentials this may be either because you may have mistyped your email address and/or your password or Windows Phone was not able to infer the additional information it needed to connect. Let's assume you are connecting into a Microsoft Exchange, Office 365 or Google Apps/Gmail account, you may be prompted for an additional set of fields such as "User Name" and "Domain". Some services allow for an email and the user name not being the same. For example Microsoft products use the first part of your email (what is in front of the "@" symbol) but Google Apps/Gmail requires you to use your whole email address as your user name. The domain and server fields are required as part of your network credentials (your network domain or LAN domain) and your server name is needed in case you need to be validated by an email server sitting in a different web address. For example; Google Apps/Gmail always uses "m.google.com" as your email/credential validation server, no matter what your network domain name really is. In this case, just use the same value on both. If you press the "show all settings" button; you will be able to see some more settings that will control the behavior of your email app on your Windows Phone. I will detail your options next as it is the same place you would land if you are changing the settings for an existing account.

Changing An Existing Account: When you get to the settings for an account that has already been setup, you will only be able to change a few of the settings. Should this account not work properly, you can always remove it altogether and create a new one replacing the previous one. From your Account List, you will be able to touch one of the existing accounts. Doing so will take you to the screen where you can provide the "Account Name" which is used as the name of that "inbox" or account. The name of the account will be displayed in the tile that appears in the Home Screen; the App list and any settings page showing information for this account. "Download New Content" refers to how often you want to receive emails, notifications, and other elements. Your options are on a cycle (every 15, 30 or 60 minutes); manually, or as they arrive. The recommended setting is "as they arrive". This means that as soon as an email arrives at your email server, your smartphone will know it and let you know. Some people are used to setting their devices on a check loop (for example every 15 minutes or so); while this option is possible, it turns out this is not my recommendation because your smartphone is going to be attempting a connection 96 times a day, even when you are sleeping. The same logic stands for checking for email hourly only it would happen 24 times a day. Nevertheless, this means that even when you don't have any emails, your phone is going to be consuming data with the back and forth of checking if you have emails and if you happen to get an email 1 minute after you just checked, and you are running on an hourly loop; you will not know that a new email just arrived for another 59 minutes (risking getting urgent communication to you almost an hour too late). Manual checking will obviously minimize your bandwidth usage but you will not be advised of a new email coming in automatically and email anxiety can actually cause you to check more often than when on a loop. Using the preferred setting for "push notifications" (or "as items arrive") means that when the server receives a new email, it sends or "pushes" a note to the smartphone so that the smartphone gets the email at that point. Other fields available to you on this settings page are for "Download Email From" which lets you choose whether you want the most recent emails from your inbox downloaded or if you want all of them. Please be aware that this setting affects your inbox by default but in reality applies to all folders that you choose to keep synchronized with your email server. Choosing what content to sync will also change what type of data comes into your Windows Phone. Choosing Email, Contacts and/or Calendar will get information from the server that will end up in an inbox, the People Hub, or your calendar for this particular account. You can combine whichever types of content to sync you want or have all selected. Once an account is created; the account "User Name" cannot be changed. The "Password", however; can be changed as many different organizations have different rules about password security and frequency for changing their passwords. If you have to change your email password often, then you will most likely land on this settings page and changing the password every time your organization requires you to do so. The domain name is something that is usually not changed (just like user names) but the server where you get your emails could, so you can change this setting as well. Some servers require that you communicate with them via encrypted channels, for doing so; you need to check "Server Requires Encrypted (SSL) Connection".

- **Lock+Wallpaper**: This settings screen lets you personalize the "lock screen". The lock screen is the image that is displayed when you turn on the phone after it went into sleep mode or when it has not been used for a set amount of time. On this settings screen you can choose the image you want to display by touching the "change wallpaper" button and choosing the image of your choice. The light switch control following the button is used for indicating whether you want to display the artist image when listening to music. If you have this option turned "on"; you will see a downloaded image of the artist for whom you are listening music as long as you are listening to that artist. After your Windows Phone goes back to sleep mode (and you are still listening to music), you will be able to see the next artist's image. Your Windows Phone will go into sleep mode or will "time out the screen" in the amount of time you select in the next control. Your options are: 30 seconds, 1, 3 or 5 minutes). Additionally you are able to set a password for your Windows Phone so that when you want to return from sleep mode, only you can unlock your phone. Turning this light switch control to the "on" position takes you to a screen where you have to enter the same password twice to enable it. Once set, you can always turn this option off or leave it on for added security.

- **Location**: This is a very simple yet important settings page. All Windows Phone modules that access location based information (independent apps not included) can be turned on or off from accessing your current location with this one light switch control.
- **Cellular**: This settings page shows your cellular carrier's information plus allows for some customization in how you want to access the cellular network you normally use. Active carrier will show your current carrier. Data Connection allows you to turn on or off your data access to the carrier's broadband connection via cellular networks. If you data connection is turned on with the correspondent light switch control and you happen to be in a roaming area where your device connects to a third party roaming services provider; your Data Roaming Options will come into play. Your options here are to select "roam" or "don't roam". Roaming with data may have a different data access fee in addition to your existing fees, setting this option not to roam will prevent you from incurring any additional charges but you may have no coverage where you would otherwise have data access through roaming for a fee. The large networks in most countries have very good coverage so you would not fall into roaming, but if you are part of a small local cellular carrier, you may have to set roaming for those times you are outside of your coverage area. Check with your network carrier for coverage and your particular plan conditions. Other settings may appear here such as an "add apn" button. If you purchased your Windows Phone unlocked you may have to provide some settings on the following page, but otherwise you would not need to use these additional settings.
- **Battery Saver**: This interesting little power saver tool lets you temporarily reduce power consumption on your Windows Phone so you can extend the amount of hours of available power left on your device's batteries. This feature works in a way that it stops some of the non-essential services that are normally used but eat up your battery. Some of the services turned off with Battery saver are receiving email, apps running in the background, Wi-Fi, etc. Cell phone and text message communications are active and emails can still be sent and

received only if they are manually refreshed. In this settings page there are two checkboxes. The first one is for turning Battery Saver mode whenever the battery is considered low. If this option is selected, then Battery Saver mode is automatically turned on when your battery drops below 20%. The second checkbox is for turning Battery Saver mode on until the next time the battery receives a charge. If you happen to know you will not have access to power in an extended amount of time and will not be checking your emails periodically or do not expect them to come in, this is your best bet in extending your battery much, much longer than it normally does. At the bottom of this settings page, you will also find the remaining battery life (expressed in %) along with the estimated remaining time in hours/minutes and the amount of hours that have passed since your battery was last charged.

- **Date+Time**: This settings page allows you to set the time, change the formatting of the current time, and choose whether the current time on your Windows Phone should be synchronized with your carrier's network. The "24 hour clock" light switch control lets you display the current time in AM/PM or 24 Hour format. The "Set Automatically" light switch control lets you synchronize the clock with your local carrier's broadcast time. Turning this option to "on" will enable your Windows Phone automatically correct time and zone when you fly across time zones or when daylight savings time adjusts without you having to do anything at all. If, for any reason you set automatically to "off"; then you will be prompted to provide the following settings: time zone; date and time.

- **Brightness**: This settings page is used to change the brightness of your Windows Phone's screen. A brighter screen uses naturally more power than a dimmed out screen. However; setting your screen to always high, medium or low screen settings is too inflexible. Windows Phone devices are required to carry a light sensor that enables your device to auto-dim the screen whenever possible. This helps your Windows Phone save battery on every possible moment. Leaving the setting on the light switch control to "automatically adjust" to the "on" position will make the right decision for both visibility and battery savings all the time.

- **Internet Sharing**: This settings page will allow you to share your internet connection from your Windows Phone to any other device making your Windows Phone act like a Wi-Fi router. You will be able to turn Internet Sharing on or off with a light switch control. You will be able to set the broadcast name (what is otherwise known as network name or SSID) and then setup a password for those who connect into your device via Wi-Fi. Please be aware that your monthly bandwidth may be either capped at a maximum number of Gigabytes or you may incur into bandwidth overages. This settings page also reports to you how many users have logged into your device.

- **Keyboard**: Under the keyboard settings page you will be able to choose the keyboard language/key distribution from an extended checkbox list. At the top of this settings page you will also find a "typing settings" button that sends you to a secondary settings page where you can change the language-related behavior with a set of checkboxes for: suggest text and highlight misspelled words; correct misspelled words; insert a space after selecting a suggestion; insert a period after a double-space and to capitalize the first letter of a sentence. You can also help Microsoft by sending touch information to improve their typing technology (to make their keyboard software better). Finally you can reset the contents of the dictionary that contains the suggestions you chose.

- **Region+Language**: The changes in this settings page will take effect after you turn your phone off and on again. A Windows Phone restart can be completed by pressing the power button for several seconds until it prompts you to slide down the screen to turn off. You can power up your Windows Phone immediately after that and the changes placed in this settings screen will have taken place. On this page you can change the display language for all text and fields controlled by Windows Phone OS. Region format is the preset formatting settings for displaying dates, times, numbers, etc. Additionally, you can also change some overrides to the generic regional settings for short date, long date, what should be considered the first day of the week, locale of the system and browser & search language default language.

- **Ease of Access**: Under the settings presented in this page, you can turn from off to full your TTY/TTD mode or turn your phone's accessibility on with speech mode. The light switch for this option is turned off by default.

- **Speech**: This is the settings page for one of the most interesting and less reported on features that Windows Phone OS has. This option allows you to control your Windows Phone with speech controls. The first checkbox enables the use of speech recognition so you can press the "Windows" or "Start" hardware button at the front-center of your device (for about 1 or 2 seconds) and you can tell your device what to do. The second checkbox is used for enabling speech services even when your device is locked out therefore enabling you to listen to the content of a text message or answer it, as described in other sections of this book. Incoming text messages can be read out loud to you even with the phone locked out through specific channels such as Bluetooth, wired headset, both or to simply always read aloud your incoming messages. The default setting for this option is Bluetooth. This means that when you are connected to your device via Bluetooth, you will listen through your Bluetooth device (or your car Bluetooth connection) what the content of the message was. If you choose wired headset, only when you have your headset on, you will hear the smartphone offer to read to you the content of an incoming message. However; if you set this option to "always on" (my favorite), you will hear the ringtone for your incoming message once, then you will be offered if you want to listen to the message via speech in any situation and no matter what devices are connected to your Windows Phone. Even when there are no listening devices connected to your Windows Phone… in which case the message will be read out loud through the loudspeaker on your device.

- **Find My Phone**: The Microsoft service "Find My Phone", available to you at http://microsoft.com/windowsphone also described earlier in this book provides a way to locate your phone, ring your phone and remote-wipe your phone. To enable these features you will need to change the appropriate settings on the website, but to provide a more accurate location, you can set your device to save its location every few hours. This way when you want to find out where you left your device, it can tell what the location was for the most recent "ping". Before you even try to ring your Windows Phone. Additionally, if you want your device to connect faster to these services (therefore using more battery) you can select the checkbox.

- **Phone Update**: Every now and then your device will have a system update that will either correct bugs, enhance security, add functionality or features. You want to be prepared for this by selecting the checkboxes in this settings page. If a new update is available for your device; your Windows Phone will let you know with a popup that you can silence permanently or postpone. This notification can keep appearing every few days/weeks until you finally update your device with the new features. Updates that are of less than a specific size can be downloaded to your smartphone OTA ("over the air"). If an update is available for you, the next time you synchronize your phone with your Zune software, you will be prompted to update. You can turn these notifications off (on your Windows Phone) and you can also turn off automatic updates over the air and Wi-Fi if you are not interested in getting additional features on your device. It is highly recommended that you update as soon as you receive a notification. You will immediately benefit from fixes and new features.

- **About**: Just like on any software, there is an "about" section. In Windows Phone OS, this is it; and it displays information about your device such as: The name of the device (which you set up the first time you synchronized it with your Zune software); the model; carrier; Windows Phone OS version; total storage on your device and available storage. The "more info" button expands this section with more information about the OS and hardware software, firmware version and revisions. You can also access your device's MAC address and your SIM ID. The MAC address is a unique ID assigned to your device. This address may be needed if you need to setup your Windows Phone's access to a Wi-Fi that only allows access to devices that have declared their MAC address. Business/work Wi-Fi networks usually use separate networks for devices such as smartphones to have access to the Internet but only for employees whose MAC addresses have been provided to their administrators.

- **NOTE**: There is one more button at the end of the "About" page. The button is labeled "reset your phone". Please beware that pressing this button leads to a hardware reset of your Windows Phone that wipes it clean to factory settings. Even though the UI will confirm with you whether you are sure to reset your phone to factory settings, do not press this button unless you are willing to start setting it up from scratch.

- **Feedback**: If these settings are enabled, Windows Phone will send Microsoft information from your device about an app crashing (if such thing happened) or usage information that lets Microsoft change the way Windows Phone OS behaves so you get a more pleasant experience. You can turn off this feature if you don't want to provide this information.

Applications pivot page

- **Background Tasks**: This settings page will show you what apps are running in the background. Windows Phone allows you to multitask with all apps, but only a few are actually running in the background while another app is running in the foreground. Most apps will go into a "frozen mode" while in the background while you are not using them. The ones that are truly running in the background are those that allow you to listen to music fetch emails, post or retrieve emails/tweets and other notifications from the web, etc. If any apps that take advantage of background processing happen to be running, they will be listed in this settings page. Pressing on the "Advanced" button will take you to a list of all apps you have installed on your Windows Phone that can run while in the background.

- **Games**: This settings page lets you change how your Xbox LIVE connection behaves with the online services. There are only a few light switch controls for you to change in this page. "Connect With Xbox LIVE" allows you to upload game scores and achievements to your gamer profile; you can compare scores with your Xbox LIVE contacts when you have this light switch turned on. "Sync Game Requests" is used to enable/disable the service that automatically gets multiplayer game requests. Some games are prepared for multiple players to play at the same time from different devices; this option allows you to get game requests from the Xbox LIVE service. "Show Game Alerts" show you notifications that arrive to your device regarding your ongoing games (such as when playing by turns). When turned on, notifications are always displayed.

- **Internet Explorer**: This option in the Applications Settings allows you to set Internet Explorer to behave the way you want it to behave and it gives you the option of choosing the privacy level you want to give to it. The first option you will see is the light switch control for allowing access to your current location. Search services and other features are further enhanced by providing you with local information related to where your last known GPS location was. Next will be a checkbox for allowing cookies on your phone. If you browsed on your desktop, you probably know what cookies are. In case you don't; cookies are bits of information that the sites you visit leave on your device. For example, a site like eBay.com or Amazon.com may leave the last category you were in so that the next time you land on their webpage, it knows where to take you (instead of just taking you to the homepage every time). Some websites store more or less information about what was done when you were visiting them. The next checkbox to enable a feature is for whether you want to get suggestions from Bing as you type in the address bar. This relates to the functionality described in the address bar, where, if turned on, you will see suggestions that match what you have typed so far. I personally leave this option always checked as I prefer to type a few characters from the web address and then select the item from the drop down list that pops while I type. Next option in the settings page is another checkbox to indicate whether you want to allow Internet Explorer to collect your browsing history. Another option is what type of website preference you have: desktop or mobile. This one option is worth explaining further. Up until a few years ago, when mobile browsers were not as capable as Internet Explorer in Windows Phone and cellular data access was too expensive, companies were attempting to detect how your browser was announcing itself: a mobile browser or a desktop browser. Mobile browsers detected as such would be served pages with less information, simpler designs and would use less bandwidth to download. This meant that website developers had to develop for both mobile and desktop websites. The fully functional desktop version would be far too complex for mobile browsers. Nowadays with the browsers provided in all major mobile platforms this is becoming less of a problem, so website developers are not required to do double the work, even though some still do for backward compatibility. For one, bandwidth is much more affordable and the other browsers have become almost as capable as their desktop counterparts.

Back to the settings page; this option will let you choose how you want your Internet Explorer to identify itself when downloading a webpage. Personally, I prefer to leave the browser in Desktop mode. Yes, I certainly use more bandwidth, but I get to see the fully functional website of what I am looking for. It also means that most of the time I have to zoom in to see what the webpage says because the fonts being used may be too small, but it is a price I am willing to pay. If you choose the mobile browsing mode and the site in question does not have one, you will still see the full version, but if they have a mobile version you will end up getting a faster webpage that does not require zooming in to get to the information you want. The next item in the settings page is whether you want links from other apps that link into a webpage to open Internet Explorer in a new tab or if you want to use the current tab. Using the current tab you run the risk of losing the webpage you were browsing in before some other app opened a link and Internet Explorer moved on to the new page. Finally, there is a Delete History button for deleting the stored bits and pieces of websites that are kept in your device after browsing, including the name and web address of the sites you visited.

- **Maps**: This settings page lets you change the way in which the Maps app behaves and reacts to your input. These are pretty considerable changes in behavior, you can make your app change behavior from your typical mapping tool to a tool that lets you talk and interact with it via voice commands. The first option light switch allows you to "Read Directions Aloud When Tapping". When you have this option turned on, the app will "talk to you" through the steps you need to take to get somewhere. The following two-option radio button allows you to choose whether the map should always have North on the top of the screen or if the top of your screen should be the direction in which you are currently moving. The third control is called "Use My Location" and when turned on allows your Windows Phone to use location information when the mapping app requests it. This information is ultimately used in services such as "Local Scout" and the "Local" pivot page that shows relevant results in the area where your Windows Phone is located. Finally, there is a "Delete History" button that lets you remove all device-stored information for mapping. This delete includes previous searches, pins and image information that had been cached on your device for faster displaying.

- **Messaging**: The messaging settings page can be accessed from within the Messaging app by going into the menu and selecting the Settings option just as you can go into the Settings app, and then selecting Messaging from the Applications pivot page. In this page you can select whether you want to have access to Facebook chat or not by turning on/off the "Facebook chat" light switch. When turned on, you will be connected to Facebook chat and your status (available, busy, away, appear offline, etc.) will be determined based on the last status you set for your chat status. "Group text" allows you to group-send messages in a way that you don't need to send the message to each member of that group. This option also helps keep replies in a single thread by using MMS. The button to change your "SMS Center Number" is related to your carrier and how it handles the exchange of text messages between mobile devices and its own network. If you purchased your device from a cellular carrier, then you don't need to change this setting. If you bought your device unlocked or from a different but compatible network, you will need to update this value. Please make sure you update the number while you have a support rep on the phone or take the device to an authorized retailer for updating this information if your SMS, text and MMS messages are not working.

- **Music+Videos**: The settings page for Music+Videos has only two settings you can choose from. "Connect With Zune" light switch will enable/disable whether your device will get information from the Zune site and download the latest information about the author/singer playing at that time along with image(s) of the group that is playing the current song. The second setting is a checkbox to let your device know whether it should download any new podcasts whenever Wi-Fi happens to be available. Additionally, you will notice a link into your "Zune Account Settings". This link takes you to the webpage where you can change your Zune settings (which you can also do from your desktop). You may need to enter your Live/Passport credentials to log into this webpage if you setup Internet Explorer not to remember passwords.

- **Office**: One would think that there are more settings to Office on your Windows Phone than there really are… In this settings page you can enter your name or initials that will identify your changes when you edit documents, make comments, add notes and documents are set up for tracking changes. You will also find a checkbox for opening SharePoint within the Office hub plus the required fields for connecting into your corporate/personal SharePoint service. Finally, you will also see a button to "Reset Office". Please be careful with this button as it will delete all your documents stored on your device and will reset your Windows Phone Office settings back to factory default. This will not remove any synchronized copies you may have online.

- **People**: This settings page allows you to control how your Windows Phone handles your contacts in the People hub. The most prominent items in this settings page are the two buttons you can press at the top of the page. The first button is called "Import SIM Contacts"; and is enabled if your device has a SIM card and it contains a contact list. You could move your contacts from an old cell phone by copying them into your SIM card, and then from your SIM card into your new Windows Phone. The second button is called "Filter My Contact List"; and when pressed you are taken to a page where you can choose the accounts you want to be used as source of contact information that you can later on integrate. You will be offered a list of all your email services (if you have accounts connecting into more than one) plus you will have access to your Facebook, LinkedIn, and Twitter accounts. In the future; when Microsoft expands into more social networks, they will be listed in here as well. My recommendation to you is to leave all your accounts as source for contact information except Twitter because you have no control over who follows you or not on Twitter. In other words; if you have a friend on Facebook or a contact on LinkedIn and that contact shares their contact information with his/her friends; that means that you won't have to enter that contact into your Windows Phone. One of the great things about this settings is that even when you search for contacts, you will still find those contacts when you execute a search (even if you haven't checked them in this list). You also will have a chance to select whether to show updates in the several hubs where feeds from your friends are displayed when you check "Only Show Posts From People Visible In My Contact List". You can also choose how you want to have your contacts sorted (by first name or last name) and how you want them displayed (again; by first name-last name or last name-first name). Some services will allow you to find nearby places and "check in". If you want those services to access your location, you can turn on the light switch for "Use My Location". You also have the ability to save places you've checked in into your device's history to improve search results with your preferences, ratings and other information. Additionally; you also have access from this same settings page to your accounts (email and social networks) in case you need to change any information about those accounts.

- **Phone**: This settings page shows your phone number and other settings. At the top of the page you will see "My Phone Number"; this is your own cell phone number. The following control is a button with the actual phone number that your carrier requires you to call when you are picking up voicemails. If you purchased your Windows Phone from your current carrier; there will be no need to change this number, but if you purchased your device unlocked or you are bringing your device from a competing carrier; you will have to change it. Please call your carriers' customer services or technical support for further steps. Then you will have the option of selecting what to do when your outgoing calls reach the targeted number; particularly whether you want to display your own Caller ID on the target phone. Your options are "Everyone", "No One" and "My Contacts"; where the first option displays your number to everyone you call; the second never displays your number and the last option shows your caller ID only to numbers in your own contact list. The "Call Forwarding" light switch option allows you to forward your calls to a given number. The "International Assist" light switch option helps you automatically correct some common mistakes when attempting to dial international numbers or when abroad dialing into national numbers. Finally; the light switch for "SIM Security" allows you to set up a password for your SIM card to prevent usage or access should it get lost or stolen.

- **Pictures+Camera**: The settings available on this screen allow you to change the behavior of some features related to the camera and pictures in general. Most of these options are presented to you in the form of a light switch control that you can turn on or off. "Tap Screen To Take Pictures" allows you to take a picture by touching the area of the screen where you want to set the focus. The camera shutter will attempt to set focus as fast as possible on the area of the screen where you tap. "Press And Hold Camera Button To Wake Up The Phone" when this option is set to on; you can take your Windows Phone from your pocket while long-pressing the camera button to wake up the phone and open the camera app. "Prevent Accidental Camera Launch When Phone Is Locked"; If your device is locked, you are prevented from opening the camera app by pressing the camera button. This option should normally be turned off so you can get from pocket to picture in a fraction of the time you would normally take with other devices. "Include Location Info In Pictures You Take"; turning this option on saves additional data on your pictures that geographically locate the place where the picture was taken. "Keep Location Info On Uploaded Pictures"; some websites allow for the location service to be included with your pictures, this option allows/prevents that information to be uploaded. "Automatically Upload To SkyDrive"; this option allows for an immediate backup of your pictures into SkyDrive. Please note that the copies stored in SkyDrive are not at full resolution to reduce the bandwidth you use when they are uploaded. "Quick Share Account", additionally to automatically upload; you will find in the camera app menu an option to "upload to [social network name]". This option is for quickly uploading the picture into the option you select here (Facebook, SkyDrive, and Twitter). Whichever you normally use the most should be selected, this way you can upload into your preferred social network with only two clicks after you take your pictures. Finally, the "Reset Camera" button will reset your camera settings back to its default values.

- **Radio**: This settings page contains only a selection control so you can choose the country in which you are using your device as an FM radio. Depending on the country selected there might be slight variations in the preset frequencies and lower and upper boundaries in the FM range.

- **Search**: This settings page is meant for configuring all you can do with the Search app. The light switch at the top of the page allows you to turn on or off the use of location services by providing your current location. Local search results are provided when you enable this option. Sending information for Microsoft tags (when the search app scans and sends information about a Microsoft Tag/equivalent to a bar code). Some Microsoft Tags require that you provide your current location and based on that information can make different offers or services. When this information is not provided you are most likely sent to a generic service that may or may not have all the elements offered in the Microsoft Tag you are scanning. Allowing the search button from the lock screen enables you to quickly jump from a locked phone into Bing. Please note that you cannot wake up your Windows Phone with this button. You first need to wake up your device and then while still locked press the search button. Getting suggestions from Bing while you type displays a drop down with the most likely matches for the text that you have so far. Allowing Microsoft to store and use images from your Vision searches allows Microsoft the ability to correct and enhance their search algorithms. Deleting the history with the "Delete History" button removes all search data stored so far such as previously-typed search terms, searches executed with Vision and Music searches in the search app.

Chapter 9: The Windows Zune Software

The Windows Zune Software is an application for your desktop that allows you to manage all your media files on your desktop but at the same time; it allows you to have whichever files you want transferred to your Windows Phone devices. It is as much a media player as it is a management tool for your smartphone.

On your desktop, you will be able to listen to music, view videos, select and download podcasts, video podcasts and execute the purchase of any of these mentioned items. At the same time, you will use your Zune software for backing up all the content stored on your Windows Phone and upgrading your Windows Phone whenever there are updates available for your device.

In future versions of Windows Phone, you may not need to use the Zune software at all, but in any case, while you have a Windows Phone device prior to version 8 you will use Zune for these services.

Setup

In order to setup the Zune Software on your desktop (or the Mac connector if you are using a Mac) you need to open your browser and go to http://www.zune.net The webpage that will load will have a few links, but you will find a section that reads "Get Started With Zune"; the first link after that (highlighted as Step "1 Get The Zune Software") is where you need to click. The browser will take you to the "Download Zune Software" webpage. On this page you can either sign up and download or just download the installer. Click on one of those two options and follow the instructions to get the software installed. When you first click for downloading the software, you will be prompted if you want to save or run the download. Please click on the "Run" button. The installer will download and then start the installation immediately after that. Please note that you will download a large file (about 100Mb). Depending on your connection's bandwidth you may have to wait until the download completes. Once the Installer starts running, you will be prompted if you want to allow the program to make changes on your computer, please answer yes. You will then be prompted to accept the terms and conditions for using the software, please answer yes. Keep following the prompts until your Zune software is fully installed. Once the installation completes; you will be prompted if you want to launch Zune Software or close; please click on Launch.

The Zune software is now installed but it needs to find your media so it knows from where to play, and transfer media files to your Windows Phone. You will be offered an option to skip settings and start playing immediately. Let's choose the Settings option.

Setting up Zune's options is easy, you can leave all folders set to their defaults and choose the other few settings such as displaying duplicate entries if it finds the same exact song in multiple folders, etc. Click Next after selecting your preferences.

Now you are presented with a screen where you can choose what media files to show with the Zune software. You can pick and choose, or simply click on "Select All" and click Next. Keep following the prompts and you will reach the end of the wizard.

Zune Software Navigation

You will be able to find yourself at home when using this software as it uses many of the already known components included in the Metro UI that Windows Phone already uses. You will find a list on the top of your screen where you will have the main functions to choose from: quickplay, collection, marketplace, social, phone (this last option will appear after you installed Zune Software and connected your Windows Phone and it was recognized by your desktop)

Quickplay is a quick and graphical way to browse your most recent (and most played) media. **Collection** is the list of all your media. You will find that a set of subtitles will appear under Collection listing the media types. These are all the media files that exist on your desktop: music, video, pictures, podcasts, channels. **Marketplace** is where you will be able to purchase any type of media (from music, to TV, movies, video clips, podcasts and channels. Purchasing does not necessarily mean that you are paying for those products as some of them are offered for free; purchasing is the action of selecting and downloading a media file to your desktop or device. Once you sign into your account (use the Live/Passport account you already have activated for your Windows Phone), you will be able to see the features under **Social**. Finally, **Phone** offers a similar view as the collection section does, only showing what you already have on your Windows Phone. From there you can choose to send to the desktop by "syncing" your media, pictures taken or any other components that are listed under phone.

Connecting with your Phone

When you connect your phone to your desktop via a USB cable or complete a wireless connection; the Zune software starts up automatically and executes an automatic sync. When this happens; all your pictures and videos taken with your Windows Phone will be backed up to your desktop at full resolution and will become part of your "Collection - Pictures". You will then be able to access them via the Zune software or just by browsing to the folder where they are saved. Disconnecting your Windows Phone device turns the Phone section off. Whenever you connect again, the software continues the sync process where it left off.

Once in the Zune software, you can go to Phone. The landing page is the "Summary" page where you can see the progress of your sync, how much space is used on your device by media, apps, and other components along with how much available space you have left on it. Going to the other sections (Music, Videos, Pictures and Podcasts) will show you what you have on your Windows Phone and lets you manage those files. You can remove files from your device while you still have those files on your collection. If you choose a few files to be sent to your Windows Phone from your collection, please remember that those files still need to be transferred. The software initiates the sync process immediately and sends those files to your device. A few files take a few seconds to transfer, but a few Gigabytes worth of media will take a few minutes. Additionally, you can setup your device to sync with your desktop over Wi-Fi. If you set this option up; whenever your desktop is running, your Windows Phone is charging and idle, and both connected to the same Wi-Fi network, they will keep everything in sync. This comes extremely handy when you set it all up beforehand and when you get home and set your Windows Phone to charge, it will start syncing automatically, sending a copy of the pictures you took during the day into your desktop without you doing anything at all.

Zune Software Settings

The settings section of the Zune software is available through the link on the top right "settings" link. The Settings section is divided into sub-sections for Software, Phone and Account. The Phone section will not be available to you unless you are connected to a Windows Phone.

The Software section allows you to setup the way the software behaves in general. For example, you can choose what file types to have Zune associated with, how many unopened podcasts to sync at a time, what type of media to share with your Xbox 360, how to display pictures when in slideshow mode, what skin to use, whether to rip CDs to MP3 files automatically and at what quality level, etc.

The Account section shows you what account you are setup to use with Zune, what computers and devices you are using with your Zune Music Pass (a paid subscription for listening and downloading an unlimited number of songs); your purchase, rental and subscription history. This history is very important in case you want to reinstall some apps you might have purchased in the past. While you will not be charged again and you can execute the install of these apps on your Windows Phone; this is where you can see the complete list of your purchases and what the name of those apps was in case you don't remember. This section is where you can purchase Microsoft points, a Zune Pass, edit your billing options, add credit card(s), change your Zune.net profile, and many administrative tasks.

The Phone section is the main area for changing how Zune software works with your Windows Phone. Sync options will let you setup what to automatically sync to your Windows Phone. You can even setup Zune so that the songs you don't like and highlight with a broken heart are not synced to your Windows Phone and these other settings:

- Your Windows Phone has a **name**. If you are part of a household with a single computer and many Windows Phones, you will want to identify what to sync with each device. Simply name your devices in a way that you will not confuse them. From that point on, your device will be called with the new name and that name will show when it is syncing with your desktop.
- Zune can **update your device**. Going into the Update section will have the Zune software check online for updates pending for your Windows Phone. I will

explain the update process further in this chapter, but you can start the update process while in this section. Please make sure that your device is charged when updating your Windows Phone, there are steps in the update process that may take more than a few minutes and will require that you use the battery even if you are connected to your desktop via USB. After the update process completes for the first time, you will find that you have an automatic backup of your device available for you to restore if the update does not satisfy your needs. You can restore to a copy of exactly the way your device was setup at the time prior to the update's execution.

- Your Windows Phone can **sync via Wi-Fi**. As mentioned before you can have your device synced over Wi-Fi so you don't need to physically connect it to your desktop. Please note that some actions such as updates require a physical connection with your Windows Phone via USB. To setup wireless sync, just click on "setup wireless sync" and follow these prompts. You will be asked to confirm the network over which you want the automatic sync to happen (for example your home or work wireless network name). Only one network can be setup to be used as your automatic wireless syncing network.

- **Picture and Video** settings: you can choose the quality of the pictures and videos when they are copied to your desktop as well as whether to leave a copy on your device after they are synced.

- **Conversion settings** allows you to choose what bitrate (for music quality) to use on your device while syncing. For example, you may want to keep your music at high quality (larger file size) on your desktop but a lower quality (yet decent enough) setting for all the songs that are synced to your Windows Phone. You will end up saving precious space on your device if you do so. If you don't want to compromise on sound quality, you can keep the original quality and the sync process will not convert media.

- **Reserved Space** is used for leaving some of the storage reserved for use when receiving emails, attachments, videos and pictures you take with the device and apps you download from the marketplace.

Zune Software Updates

Every now and then, an update for the Zune software will pop up on your desktop. Please keep this software updated so that the newest features are available to you and your Windows Phone device.

Windows Phone Updates

Microsoft has updated the Windows Phone OS an average of one major update per year and several minor updates per year. On the two year life expectancy of your device, you should see at least one or two major OS updates and a few minor, so keeping your Windows Phone in sync with Zune software makes sense.

Every time you connect your Windows Phone to your desktop, the Zune software will sync and then try to check for updates. If an update is available to you, you can choose to update at that time or just sync and update later. Additionally, you will see on your Windows Phone from time to time a notification letting you know that there are updates pending for your device.

Once you have your Windows Phone charged and ready for the update process, you can come back to your desktop and start the updating process (in case it doesn't start automatically) by going into the Settings, Phone and Update options of the Zune software. At this point it will let you know it is checking for updates. Once confirmed that you have updates pending, it will ask for confirmation from you if you want to continue with this update and the process will start. Zune will let you know how many steps there are to complete the process and how many updates are there pending. Small updates take no more than 20 minutes and large updates (such as Mango, the first major update) take about 40 minutes to 1 hour.

During the update process you will not be able to take calls or answer text messages. Calls will be routed to your voicemail and text messages will not be received at the time of the update. You can always check your voicemail by calling your carrier's voicemail number if you need to.

Don't be concerned that your device is starting up several times, because this is a normal step that needs to happen as part of the update process. When the update process is done, your desktop will let you know that it has completed the process and that you can now unplug your Windows Phone from your desktop to enjoy the new features.

After the very first update process is completed; you will see an option that will become available to restore a backup. This is because upon every update; a full backup of your Windows Phone is executed. This feature will give you the option to restore to your previous state if there is something you don't like about your Windows Phone when the update completes. If your Windows Phone has several updates to run at one time, all of them will be executed in tandem and you will be able to update to the very initial state before all those updates executed. This is to minimize the amount of space that the backup takes on your desktop and in order to keep only one backup at any given time.

Chapter 10: Expand Your Windows Phone

How To Expand Your Windows Phone's Features

No matter how you use your Windows Phone, there will always be ways in which to extend its capabilities. With an ever-expanding Marketplace where you can get both free and paid apps; you are bound to find exactly what you are looking for. You will also be likely to find a few apps that make use of your device in a way that's innovative and you never even thought of.

You will find that most apps are provided free (sometimes with an ad bar at the bottom of the screen), or as a "limited trial" that will normally expire or have less functionality than the paid version. The intention of these free/trial versions is that you can see for yourself the quality level of the app before you buy it. You may find that you don't really care to remove the ad-bar from a free app if you only use the app sporadically. Developers will make a tiny profit out of advertising ad-prints and ad-clicks and a larger profit if you purchase the app. In any case, this is a win-win scenario for developers and users.

Regardless of your preference, visit the Windows Phone Marketplace and browse your way through many apps available, you will eventually find a few apps that will be worth the download.

Don't think that because apps are free or paid, they may be of better or worse quality. There doesn't seem to be a strong relationship between these characteristics. This is mainly because some really great apps that are free rely on a small ad bar that provides the developer enough income every time you use such app; therefore the app is just offered to you free of charge. Other developers offer an add-free experience where you can pay for a full version or simply use the trial version which may have less functionality or function for a limited time.

Microsoft has made and is making a huge effort in getting developers of apps that already exist in other platforms to port them into Windows Phone. Most of those development companies have already done so. You shouldn't be surprised to find the same apps in all mobile platforms including Windows Phone.

Some of the most common free and paid apps you can install on your device are:

- **Adobe Reader:** PDF documents are used across platforms both mobile and desktop, there are PDF reader apps in all major platforms and Windows Phone is one of them. You can download this reader FREE into your device and whenever you try to open an email attachment or you attempt to open a PDF on your Windows Phone, you will see this app start and show you the PDF in question on your device.
- **Amazon Kindle:** Sometimes you may find yourself in a waiting area and without an eReader (if you have one and left it at home). If you don't have an eBook reader, this may be your best approach at seeing how eBooks work in general. Even though eReader hardware is available and most people read on dedicated eReader hardware; you may want to keep your most recent books so you can pick up where you left off. Amazon Kindle is a FREE download. Having an eReader software does not mean you have to purchase eBooks. In fact; there are plenty of free "classics" available from Amazon for you to read them. I am an avid reader and whenever I have a few minutes I download my current book(s) if I don't already have them, synch to my latest read page and when I'm done; I synch back. This is an extremely low cost solution to eBooks. You don't necessarily need to have eBook reading hardware to use the software on your Windows Phone and you have access to the almost 2,000,000 pieces literature available from Amazon.
- **Amazon Mobile:** If you have an Amazon account and you normally purchase items from them, this is a great FREE way to have access to the full set of products offered by Amazon. Even if you use it only to compare prices while at a

store, you can always pull your Amazon Mobile app and compare store prices to Amazon prices.

- **Banking apps:** Having access to your bank's account information may be useful when you are away from your desktop and about to make a purchase. Do you have sufficient credit line to pay with a specific credit card? Would it be more convenient to make a payment with your debit card? Did you remember to send payment XYZ before the due date? Has that payment been charged? All these questions can be answered while you are out and about and with FREE apps from your bank. Banks charge ATM fees but they do no charge an "app fee"; you can do most of your ATM tasks right on your Windows Phone.

- **DirecTV:** Dis you remember to set your DVR to record a particular program or series? Is the game at 6 or 7 PM? This FREE app lets you control your DirecTV DVR (if you have one) or simply check listings, times and schedules from your favorite channels.

- **eBay:** People looking for a bargain, used products or sellers of such products are avid users of eBay. This FREE app from eBay lets you sign up, search, bid, follow or watch and be notified about any of your current bids and products.

- **foursquare:** This is another FREE app, in this case you can use the app to check in when you arrive somewhere and see if there are any special offers or discounts for users that have checked into that particular store.

- **GoogleDocs:** If you use Google Apps or Google Docs, you will appreciate any of the FREE apps available to you for keeping an eye on your shared documents. Any documents stored on Google's cloud can be accessed from the different clients.

- **Last.fm:** Last.fm is a FREE music streaming service that allows you to setup a particular set of musical preferences or "likes" and will create a stream of music that resembles the style and tone of those you selected. Information about the author and/or artist playing the current song/set is available on screen.

- **Level:** Your Windows Phone contains sensors that can be used to determine the spatial position and orientation of your device. One such set of sensors, called "accelerometers" are used in this FREE app where you can use your Windows Phone to place it on a surface to perfectly align a picture on the wall. The interface used is the typical bubble-level tool where you have a bubble to show you whether the item is level or not.

- **Netflix:** This FREE app allows you to both manage your movie list and to stream full length movies to your Windows Phone. Watch that episode you missed from last season or just add the new movie your friend talked to you about to your movie queue so it will be sent to you when it becomes available.

- **SkyDrive:** Access all your Office documents stored in the cloud, setup new folders and download those documents to your Windows Phone for a quick correction or simply play the PowerPoint presentation on your Windows Phone to practice that sales pitch you are about to give.

- **Astronomy apps:** Use your device's GPS location services plus its other sensors to see a celestial map. Use these apps as a guide to point your telescope in the right direction and angle. The best of these astronomy apps are paid apps.

- **Unit Converter:** Convert to and from any unit with these (mostly) FREE apps. How many liters are in 27.3 gallons? How many feet are in 172 meters? These conversions and many more are available with a few touches on your screen. Some of these apps even include currency exchange rates for international transactions. Some of these apps may be paid since they may be accessing paid services for currency exchange information.

- **Where's My Car?** This is a great FREE app that you can use while at theme parks and other venues that have a huge parking lot. After a few days of going to the venue's parking areas, they all start to look alike. For these cases, you activate it before leaving your car's side. GPS positioning is then used to save the location and when you are ready to leave the park at the end of the day, you use it as a walking GPS to guide you to your car.

- **RSS Reader:** RSS Feeds are one of the most common ways to keep up to date with news from many different sources, news and blogs. Instead of going to each of the websites you would normally visit, you set those feeds up in a service such as Google Reader on the web and then use a Google Reader client to access them from your Windows Phone. This way you can go seamlessly from your desktop to your Windows Phone and they are both kept in sync with the articles you have already read and the ones you haven't. If you normally don't read on your desktop, you can use other RSS readers that you setup on your

Windows Phone and keeps track of your read and unread articles so you can keep reading where you left off when you come back. You can find many reader apps both FREE and paid.

- **WordPress:** This is the other side of RSS readers... This FREE app lets you write content that will be published on your blog. There are other apps that will let you publish to other blog systems that may or may not be powered by WordPress.
- **YouTube:** Access an endless feed of videos with this FREE app that lets you watch/stream to your Windows Phone.

These are just a few and quick sample of the many different types of features you can access on your device. While some of these are paid apps, most of them are actually free as they assume you are already a user of those services or even hope that you may become a user of these services on your desktop.

A Windows Phone 8 Preview

Software is a never ending list of enhancements and fixes. Windows Phone is great as it is, but there are always new features to add. No matter where those enhancements come from (they can be new ideas or functionality implemented by competing software), there's always room for improvement.

All the features we have reviewed in this book are available to you in Windows Phone 7.5 and will be also available in future versions of Windows Phone.

Enter Windows Phone 8; codename "Apollo"; is scheduled to be released at a date close to the release of Windows 8 (which is to be released in August-October 2012).

The main changes in Windows Phone 8 will be under the hood and most likely invisible to most users. These changes will not affect compatibility or usability other than running faster, leaner, better. On the visible side of changes, you will start to notice that Windows Phone 8 devices will be able to come in 4 different resolution sizes with more form factors (keyboard, sliders, etc.). The compatible services will also be expanded and made even more consistent with their desktop counterparts.

Some key features to be expected in Windows Phone 8 will be:

- **MSIE10m (Internet Explorer 10 mobile):** The new version of Microsoft's browser, to be included in Windows 8, will also be included in the next version of Windows Phone. Just like MSIE9 in Windows Phone 7.5, it will be a very optimized version that will support the latest web technologies.
- **Camera Enhancements:** A better camera experience will be offered that will include "lens apps" that can be used to alter the picture in real time and allow for further expansion into creative apps that make use of these features.
- **Local Scout Expansion:** will also include personalized recommendations. This item is not clearly described so far, but more details will be made public about it soon.
- **Skype:** While Skype app was released in early 2012; there will be further integration with the OS since, Skype can be considered an additional social network that can be used to chat, make video and voice calls, Skype to Skype client calls (free) or Skype calls into phone numbers all around the world for a low fee. The inclusion of front-facing cameras in 2012 allows for easy setup of video calls. Additionally, the chat integration can be provided in the messaging hub. However, there are some conflicting reports at this time that also indicate that carriers may choose not to provide this particular feature on all their Windows Phones.
- **Further SkyDrive Integration:** Your content will become available through SkyDrive to all of your platforms. SkyDrive will essentially become a common way to exchange information between all your devices while at the same time being able to store a copy of it in the cloud as a backup. What you can do today with Windows Phone 7.5 and its Office apps, your contacts and auto uploading your pictures, will be expanded to many more apps and services while you still use a desktop or a tablet. It is expected that SkyDrive will eliminate (or come close to eliminate) the need to use a computer to synchronize your Windows Phone with your desktop(s).
- **Wallet and NFC:** Included in Windows Phone 8 will be the ability to use hardware that supports NFC (Near Field Communications) and wallet services. The wallet integration into Windows Phone 8 will allow managing many cards. NFC is the technology behind secure communications at a very short distance to

be used for payment at point of sales. This means No more wallets full of cards, all of them can be used from your smartphone by selecting on your device what card to use for payment. Some subway stations already support this payment methods and it is just a matter of time until all points of sale support this form of payment.

- **App-to-App Communication:** Windows Phone 7 and 7.5 isolates apps from communicating with each other as a security measure. Windows Phone 8 will offer a secure way to communicate between apps that will not put at risk the integrity of either app's data. This will allow for two apps share information when needed and be able to feedback each other.
- **Data Smart:** This is a way to intelligently decide what, how and when to reduce your bandwidth helping you to avoid a big surprise and overages when your cell-phone bill arrives home every month.
- **Business-Level Features:** The whole device will be encrypted and supported with hardware accelerated encryption making it very hard for anyone that gets a Windows Phone 8 access the information within. Inclusion of secure boot in a similar implementation to Windows 8. Ability to distribute Windows Phone 8 apps to all phones that belong to a particular business. Account and security policies will be supported to actively enforce security for compliance with many security standards.
- **Multicore Processor support:** Processors with more than one core will now be supported for manufacturers that want to include them. This requirement is seen as a natural evolution as more features make the OS more complex and requiring of more processing power. Note that contrary to other OSs, previous versions of Windows Phone 8 never required processors with more than a single core because its operation is so smooth. Adding multiple core support to an OS that does not require it, simply means that it will burn through the battery faster as many Android OS and the iPhone 4S normally do.
- **Shared Components with Windows 8:** The main core components of Windows 8 will also be ported to Windows Phone 8, making your smartphone more in line with your desktop technology as well as with the new ARM Windows 8 tablets.
- **Consistent Experience with all platforms:** A very similar experience will be offered across platforms: Windows Phone 8, Windows 8, cloud services and the

next version of Xbox. Synchronization will happen through a new client (not Zune software) allowing to share music, video, pictures, etc. across all environments while sharing content between all of them; including games, entertainment, etc.

Want To Learn More?

If you are interested in more information about the user and extension of your Windows Phone or if you want to read news and tricks you can do on your Windows Phone, please visit my blog.

http://www.gadgetix.com

In my blog I write about gadgets in general, but I center my comments and editorials around the technologies I use the most; Windows Phone being one of the top subjects.

Thank you for reading this book

www.ingramcontent.com/pod-product-compliance
Lightning Source LLC
Chambersburg PA
CBHW080413060326
40689CB00019B/4231